# DIVINE INCUBATION

## PREREQUISITE FOR LIFE AND MINISTRY

**Divine Incubation:**
Prerequisite for Life and Ministry


ISBN 978-978-769-913-3

Published in Nigeria by:
**CHRISTLINE BOOKS & PUBLICATION**



*For further information or permission, address:*

**CHRISTLINE BOOKS & PUBLICATION**
77a, Bola Ahmed Tinubu Road, Iju-Ishaga, Lagos, Nigeria.
08033005279, 08094633988

isaacohi@hotmail.com

**All Scriptures are from the New King James Version (NKJV) of the Bible, except otherwise stated.**

# Contents

# Dedication

This book is dedicated to my daughter, **Abimbola Mojolaoluwa Ohiozua**, currently residing in Toronto, Canada. Despite facing health challenges, she is resolute in her commitment to live for the Lord and bring humanity blessings. Her life has inspired numerous young individuals in Nigeria and North America. I pray that her lifestyle and character will continue to ignite revival and spiritual reforms within families and nations. Amen.

# Acknowledgment

I give glory to God from Whose hand we have received mercy upon mercy to be part of His move in these last days.

This book wouldn't have been birthed without the willingness of many brethren who yielded their lives to the truth of the word of God even when it appeared hard. We proved the authenticity of His word together. Their number is too great to list comprehensively.

I must also acknowledge my wife, Wuraola Ohiozua. She has always been the silent force encouraging me to pursue the tasks God has entrusted into my hands. Her roles as a wife and mother are invaluable; she is a pillar of support for me, our daughter, and the other children God has blessed us with.

Thank God for the unwavering commitment of Olugbenga Odepase who has become a treasure to my life and ministry. As Timothy was to Paul so he is to me in the ministry. He labored tirelessly from the transcribing to publishing. His labor over this work is priceless. Angela, his wife contributed her quota in her little way. May the Lord reward both of you eternally beyond your wildest imagination. Amen.

# Preface

This book in your hand – **"Divine Incubation: Prerequisite for Life and Ministry"** is a burden that came immediately after *"Crafted in Christ"*, our first work published a few years ago.

Several attempts were made to swiftly put this work together to discharge the burden in print. I would say it took longer than envisaged. As expected, many challenges immediately sprang up just like the first work but the Lord came through for us again.

All the messages compiled herein are a few of the utterances God brought to His people as I preach from place to place; the issues God confronted us with are still fresh in my heart and I have not recovered from them. God wanted it to have effects on my life and ministry before publishing them. I kept holding it in the place of prayer!

You will discover in this brief book that God has no problem shooting forth His people like arrows to do irrecoverable damage in the camp of His enemies. Still, the issues have always been ***"Are they ready and sufficiently sharpened to undertake such a delicate but honorable task"?*** The urgency of the need to get His counsel done on planet Earth won't inundate God to make Him compromise the necessary incubation which is a prerequisite for all that will be sent. Should the wicked one spot "buts" in the disciples' life; he will by no means show mercy until he becomes a reproach to the Master.

As you read through, feel free to drop the book to pray anytime you sense the Holy Spirit leading you to do so. The truth you will encounter here is not to condemn you but to tune your heart to seek God until you have truly become the beloved of the Lord.

**OHIOZUA A. ISAAC**
September 2024

CHAPTER
*1*

# Dealing with Your "Buts" Through REST

*"Behold, the Lord's hand is not shortened, that it cannot save; nor His ear heavy, that it cannot hear. But your iniquities have separated you from your God; and your sins have hidden His face from you, so that He will not hear. For your hands are defiled with blood, and your fingers with iniquity; your lips have spoken lies, your tongue has muttered perversity. No one calls for justice, nor does any plead for truth. They trust in empty words and speak lies; they conceive evil and bring forth iniquity."* Isa 59:1-4

See what God is saying in the scripture above: 'No matter where you are and whatever condition you are in, My hand can reach you. There is nowhere that My hand cannot get to, no matter how narrow, shallow, deep, or even inaccessible that place seems. There is no situation that I cannot touch or change. My ears are wide open because I love to hear those who seek Me out.

Even though it has not become a spoken word, every thought is loud enough in His ears. He can see near, far, even amid thick darkness; He doesn't need a microscopic lens to see the tiniest things. He sees clearly into the secret places. It is nothing for God to save one or many; no matter how desperate and bad your situation may be. He loves to deliver those who turn to Him in their helplessness (Matt 11:28, Jn. 6:37).

But there is a 'but' in verse two of Isaiah 59 that I need you to pay particular attention to. I wish the 'but' didn't appear at all. What does 'but' signify in the light of the above passage? The 'but' represents a hindrance or stumbling block to progressing with God. It indicates a deviation from what should be the ideal. It is a complete departure from what is good and desirable. When you get into the heart of God, it seems as though God is groaning and sighing because of this 'but'.

God knows that it is practically impossible to build anything that will last when this 'but' is in place in a person's life. So, what is this 'but' that God is referring to? It is your iniquities! Iniquity is the nature or lifestyle that is not fully aligned with the glory of God and does not fully reflect godliness in your life. It is a life that completely deviates from God's expectations for a person. (For clarity's sake, I will use 'iniquity(ies)' interchangeably with 'but' and vice versa. Please note that they have the same meaning in this context).

Your but is not a friend but an enemy to your soul. Every but you allow to subsist in your life is like nurturing an eventual downfall. All but has its root in sin; it is sin that empowers every but! What normally makes God turn His back against any man, family, nation or generation is this 'but'. God cannot stand sin and iniquity! The size or degree of sin is insignificant; every sin is an abomination before the Lord. Anytime God sees even the 'tiniest' of sins, He mobilizes Himself against it. His nature cannot tolerate any form of sin.

> *"Your eyes are too pure to look on evil; you cannot tolerate wrongdoing..."* **Hab. 1:13** - NIV

## Your First Approach

The solution to any problem at all starts with identifying and admitting there is a problem. Until you have done a sincere assessment and thorough examination of your life, your deliverance tarries, applying pomades of hypocrisy will not make the problem vanish. A lack of knowledge will make you cover up a problem. To cover up or feign all is well is to scrap the help of God that would have readily come to you.

> *"If you cover up your sin you'll never do well. But if you confess your sins and forsake them, you will be kissed by mercy."* **Prov. 28:13** - TPT

Call it what it is; don't dress up your 'but'. Take responsibility, and you will receive help. *"...But your iniquities..."* and not another's. You can keep all the other commandments, but if you fail in one, in the eyes of the Lord, you are guilty of all. Can I ask you what that 'but' is that has been weighing you down over the years? Will you be humble enough to uncover it before the Lord so it can be dealt with? Do not make excuses or indulge yourself. If you continue to do so, it indicates you are not ready for divine help and deliverance.

Your *but* could be that anger, for another it could be this strong appetite for fashion, sex, clothes, cars, money, and the like. When are you going to rest from sinning? Ananias and Saphira didn't pay attention to their inner weakness until it found them out. You may think lying is not so serious a sin, but that was what buried this couple. They pretentiously lied to the Holy Ghost and they paid dearly for it. It was not compulsory to sell their land if they had problems laying down all of the proceeds. Their own 'but' received instant judgment! I hope you will not continue to pretend as if all is well when you know it has not been well between you and your Lord. The solution to your *buts,* no matter how varied, lies with the rest God has provided.

## Come to His Rest

> *"Come to Me, all you who labor and are heavy laden, and I will give you rest.*
> *Take My yoke upon you and learn from Me, for I am gentle and lowly in heart, and you will find rest for your souls. For My yoke is easy and My burden is light."* **Matt. 11:28-30**

God is more than willing to have His children enter into His rest. A life that is void of continuous harassment from the enemy and the world system is what God wishes for all men. But then, this precious and victorious life won't just come to anyone by merely wishing for it; it must be through certain and unmistakable actions.

To be free from the hustling and bustling that men have been conditioned into by the very nature they bear, something has to happen to you inwardly. God's rest is obtainable but not automatic. There is something you must do to enter into it. Life itself is a battleground and as such, not everyone survives the attendant assaults. If you want to be free from your 'buts', discovering God's rest is not optional.

So, what does rest mean? It is a state of freedom from activity or labor according to Webster's Dictionary. It is freedom from anxieties, exertions, toils, disturbances, etc. I don't think there is anyone who doesn't like to have rest from oppositions or challenges life throws at him or her. Even a wicked man likes not to be opposed! No one can amount to anything tangible as far as God's purpose is concerned when rest is absent in his or her life. The rest I am talking about only comes from God. It cannot be achieved single-handedly by yourself! Christ is the Author and giver of true rest. He alone has the inroad to it. Did you know that all the troubles and unrest we see in the world today only point to the scarcity of rest among men? It is not that the world has not invested enormous efforts to secure rest, but they have looked in the wrong direction. Both local and international humanitarian organizations have honestly and are still laboring to bring about rest in the world, but all to no avail.

> *"For when they say, "Peace and safety!" then sudden destruction comes upon them, as labor pains upon a pregnant woman. And they shall not escape."* 1 Thess. 5:3.

Suffice it to say that, as popular and commanding as money appears to be, it cannot afford a jot of rest. An abundance of material resources won't achieve it either; the more material possessions, the more rest becomes elusive. Look at the story of the *young rich ruler* in *Mk. 10:17-22*. The Bible recorded that he had great possessions. Despite all those 'blessings,' he was always on the run, needing something greater than affluence to permanently settle his unsettlement.

When he finally met Jesus, the Author of rest, he couldn't obey what he was told to do all because of the magnitude of what he had as possessions. He had his possessions intact as he went away, however, sorrowfully. So, when rest eludes a man, it is not because he doesn't have enough money; it is because money is too poor to afford rest!

Rest is the absence of inner agitation and dissatisfaction common to man. People run up and down, taking up unimaginable ventures just to get some sort of security or a sense of personal achievement. Yet they lack contentment despite huge possessions to their name. Don't be tempted either, to think rest is affirming mediocrity. It has nothing to do with an immobilized and lazy disposition. Rest is ensued when you have deliberately yoked your life with Christ both for learning and living. Christ's way of life is the true meaning of rest!

When a man has contracted this rest, he is free from corruption and the hollowness that characterizes the nature of every man irrespective of color and race. Such a man now has a correct understanding that:

> *"...it is not of him who wills, nor of him who runs, but of God who shows mercy."* Rom.9:16

Let me say to you again, nothing else can fill the void inherent in every soul other than the presence of God. The more of Him in your life, the more Spirit-empowered effectiveness and productivity you will know. (See also John 15:5).

Jesus came purposely because of our sins. There was no reason for Him to have come if no man can be freed from his buts. The reason why many still struggle with sin is that they lack a functional understanding of what being in Christ means. They have often come to embrace religion and not life. Many erroneously think that Jesus is a divine force that has come to push their desires into reality. They are mistaken! Until Jesus has become your only reason for living, you cannot experience true rest.

You have known rest when your living is about only one thing – growing in the knowledge of Christ. It means God has helped you to be completely satisfied with and in Jesus. This satisfaction I am talking about goes beyond empty profession and pretense. We have a host of believers whose cravings and longings for the world are inconceivable. They seem loyal to anything and everything that will promote self but not Jesus. The fact that people fill our church auditoriums, shouting and dancing around Jesus, does not equate to rest.

God years for people in whose hearts He is truly the Lord. Make no mistake in thinking you are faithful to God when you are double-minded. You cannot have your loyalty split between Christ and the world and claim you have known rest. That would be a complete falsehood. There is no room for lukewarmness; you are either cold or hot. Rest is when you have truly come to the end of personal ambition and have clearly set your affection on your Lord. When Christ has not become your main and only trophy (reward) to show men, you will often fall prey to the ceaseless seductions from the enemy's quarters.

As soon as you practically choose Christ as your teacher and pattern for living, you are now treading the path to total victory over sin and hell. This is the truth that the devil is working tirelessly to conceal from many. As you learn Christ, there is a lifting and repositioning of your life from the company of the dead. (Phil. 3:8). It is the power of Christ residing in your life that makes you insurmountable by the power of darkness. There could be several attempts on your life by adversities, but as long as you are abiding, you can never be rooted out.

It is only in Christ that there is freedom from sin. What a relief to be free from the pangs of unrighteousness! You will not know the depth of God's manifold glory until you are clearly outside the region of sin. The reason you fall in and out of sin could be your inability to see or savor your Lover's (Jesus) incomparable affection. The seductions thrown at you from the world system seem effectual since the condition of your heart remains unstable. It takes a person who is ruthless with sin to enjoy rest in every facet of life.

Have you truly bid farewell to sin and all forms of unrighteousness? As I study I Jn. 3:4-6 over and over again, it seems to me that if any man will sin at all, he will have to come out of Christ to be able to do so. There is no sin to commit in Jesus. The secret to a daily victorious living is abiding in Christ. To abide is to have your being deeply rooted in Christ. Those whose being is superficial are subject to all kinds of drifting. There is grace flowing from God to every one of us to say NO to sin!

Those who know God do not make sin a practice. Yes, you may fall into sin, but it is outrightly abnormal for a Christian to live in sin. The only way to be free from the guilt and grasp of sin is to genuinely repent and turn away from that sin. The finest perfumes are unable to eliminate or mask the foul odor generated by sin in a person's life. Sin cannot be concealed indefinitely; it will inevitably come to light one way or another.

> *"You will never succeed in life if you try to hide your sins. Confess them and give them up; then God will show mercy to you."* **Prov. 28:13** - GNB

Sin seeks to enslave and make the one who commits it a captive. No one makes real progress when they are a captive. Sometimes, the one who has been crippled by sin may appear to be moving, but not all movements are upward. There are individuals whose movements are downward. The word of God admonishes us not to envy evildoers (sinners) because they shall soon be cut down (Psalm 37:1-2). Let me tell you that everyone whose heart has not departed from sin does not have a portion in the coming glory.

It may seem like the issue of sin is being overly emphasized. The reason is that it is fundamental, and if not addressed, the ultimate rest that Christ is calling us into remains uncertain or elusive. The devil knows that the greatest of all burdens is sin and that nothing solidifies when sin is dominant in a person's life. Therefore, the first thing the Lord Jesus wants to remove from anyone's neck is the yoke (burden) of sin.

> *"Come to Me, all you who labor and are heavy-laden and overburdened, and I will cause you to rest. [I will ease and relieve and refresh your souls.]"* **Matt. 11:28** - AMP

It is when this ease and relief has taken place that real progress in discipleship (learning of Christ) can be made. No man can truly become a follower of Christ with his baggage of sin; he has to first be delivered from the tyranny of sin. Otherwise, he is weighed down and pinned.

No matter how well you feed a lizard, it can never become a crocodile because it has no potential of becoming one. Similarly, no matter the amount of discipleship principles applied or taught to a sinner, it cannot work. At best the sinner becomes a refined sinner. It is the new life received at new birth that has the potential to grow into Christlikeness when exposed to practical discipleship. It would be futile to bother a sinner with the issue of following in Christ's steps. (I Cor. 2:13-14).

I have heard people say it's difficult to live holy in a place like Lagos (a city in Nigeria) because of human activities within it. This is incorrect; the life of Christ is livable anywhere in the world, regardless of how thick the darkness is in such places. A true Christian ought to be a beacon of light, shining amid darkness that has thrown the whole world into confusion.

> *"That you may become blameless and harmless, children of God without fault in the midst of a crooked and perverse generation, among whom you shine as lights in the world"* **Phil. 2:15**

> *"That you may show yourselves to be blameless and guileless, innocent and uncontaminated, children of God without blemish (faultless, unrebukable) in the midst of a crooked and wicked generation [spiritually perverted and perverse], among whom you are seen as bright lights (stars or beacons shining out clearly) in the [dark] world"* **Phil. 2:15** - AMP

> *"So that you may be innocent and pure as God's perfect children, who live in a world of corrupt and*

*sinful people. You must shine among them like stars lighting up the sky"* **Phil. 2:15** - GNB

I was driving home some years ago, and the headlight of the car then had a minor fault that made the illumination excessive. As I was negotiating a hill, unknown to me, there was a commercial motorcycle approaching from the other side, and the rider was affected by the intense light. He started yelling, and there was nothing he did not say just to insult me. So, I stopped and got out of the car. As soon as he saw me alight from the vehicle, he was ready for a fight. The man was shocked and bewildered when he discovered I purposely came down to apologize to him. I think he became sorry and was wondering why my response to all his insults should be to apologize. At that moment, he didn't know what to do, but he prostrated and apologized for all that he said.

Righteousness is possible anywhere and everywhere! Light does not conform; it only shines, illuminates, and exposes darkness. It is not surprising that darkness loathes light with great intensity. That notwithstanding, darkness is displaced, incoherent, and irrelevant whenever light is operational. If you see darkness occupying any space freely, it is either light is absent or the supposed light available has been compromised and has become darkness in itself. A man cannot be manifesting darkness and light at the same time. The manifestation of one is the absence of the other!

If you still sin, you don't know Him, and you are in darkness. There is no way you can operate in the light or as light when you still condone darkness. Sin and darkness are synonymous (1 John 1:5-7). The identity of a true Christian is that he or she has departed from the life of sin. Honestly, I wonder how people get into the church and continue to parade themselves as one of His when in reality they are handcuffed by sin. Jesus said:

> *I am the good shepherd, and I know My sheep, and am known by My own*. Jn. 10:14

Thank God for the Great Shepherd, who is all-knowing and full of compassion. He does not need to conduct a census to know how many sheep He has in His flock. As we speak, He knows those who are truly His. Those who are His are not difficult to recognize – they are led by the Spirit of Christ! I hear the Lord saying, "There are those who seemingly look as though they are in the fold, but I don't know them." What a dangerous thing! That's why you must not compare yourself to another because those who do so are not wise.

Take your journey seriously and personally with the Lord. Let no man deceive you, no matter who he may be. They may even tell you it does not matter, whereas impending judgment awaits those who are not only lawless but also encourage others to be (Matt. 5:19). These men who parade themselves as servants of God are deceivers and lead God's people astray with their unwholesome and unfounded doctrines. God says they shall not be spared! (Mal. 3:5).

They preach mammon, which lacks the least power to give men the rest that has eluded them for so long. As you hear the voice of the Lord now saying to you, *"Come to Me, take my yoke upon you and learn from Me, and you will find rest for your souls."* Don't ignore this invitation to come and learn under the Author and Giver of Rest. Bow your heart in prayer as you make a personal commitment to become His follower.

CHAPTER
*2*

## True Revival

Much has been said about revival by different authors and preachers at various times. Some have witnessed genuine revival in their generation while others have come close to it. Yet, there is also a category of men used to dryness and closed heavens. Wickedness and unrighteousness became their normal way of life. None cried out to seek God; their hearts were darkened and depraved. This is what I refer to as a dangerous age. Are we gradually returning to such an era? It is a terrible thing for people to become used to such a dispensation of rot and decadence as in the days of Sodom and Gomorrah.

Revival is not easy to come by, yet God is eager and ready to release it to those who thirst and hunger for it. Organized mighty crusades and well-attended prayer meetings won't impersonate it. It is not every 'noise' and 'crying' that heralds or announces the arrival of revival, but it cannot come and men will be oblivious to it. Its effect is reawakening and lasting on the generation it descended on.

It can only be triggered by the Spirit of God when men knock desperately at the gate of heaven in the place of intense prayer. It is not arbitrary; revival is born at the instance of men and women who understand the time, just like the children of Issachar, who know what Israel ought to do at any given time (1 Chron. 12:32). Revival comes when God has seen vessels that can carry it through; men and women in whose hearts genuine hunger and thirst for righteousness reside.

Yet, until we are encapsulated in revival, our knowledge and zeal for God remain pseudo, shapeless, and unguided. The ways of God are made prominent when true revival breaks out. Whereas, several people erroneously think that revival is signaled when the acts of God are seen everywhere. This is the error that has come upon the church in our day! God shows and trains a man in His ways when he has found favor with God. The who, why, and how of God are graciously, to an extent, released to such a man. The "ways" of God involve knowing His Person intimately!

Here, the church in the wilderness comes to mind. They were more interested in experiencing the acts of God than knowing His ways just like the church we know today. Most of the messages we hear today from our pulpits are but emphases on what God can do and not who God is. These are wines that are good only to intoxicate men with mere drunkenness unto worldliness. The revival that we must seek is not a funfair or ceremonial.

> *"I hate, I despise your feast days, And I do not savor your sacred assemblies. Though you offer Me burnt offerings and your grain offerings, I will not accept them, nor will I regard your fattened peace offerings. Take away from Me the noise of your songs, For I will not hear the melody of your stringed instruments. But let justice run down like water, And righteousness like a mighty stream."* Amos 5:21-24

So, revival is when men have truly been convicted of their sins and as a result, are seeking God earnestly in spirit and truth. There is no revival until the knowledge of God has permeated the hearts of men on the earth. I am not by any means talking of knowledge about God which is common in our day either. There is a difference between knowing about God and knowing God. The former seems to be the experience while the latter is scarce among men.

You may know about God and it may not significantly affect your way of life; it's just a mere mental awareness! People become inoculated and sometimes hardened in their hearts even when they are aware there is God. That kind of knowledge about God is not useful in any way. You can't be growing in the knowledge of God and it won't show in your entire life. The expectation of every revival is that:

> *"On Zion, God's sacred hill, there will be nothing harmful or evil. The land will be as full of knowledge of the Lord as the seas are full of water. A day is coming when the new king from the royal line of David will be a symbol to the nations. They will gather in his royal city and give him honor."* **Isa 11:9-10** - GNB

> *"They shall not hurt or destroy in all My holy mountain, for the earth shall be full of the knowledge of the Lord as the waters cover the sea. And it shall be in that day that the Root of Jesse shall stand as a signal for the peoples; of Him shall the nations inquire and seek knowledge, and His dwelling shall be glory [His rest glorious]!"* **Isaiah 11:9-10** - AMP

A revival is utterly genuine when it emphasizes the oneness of the Body of Christ. Any religious or spiritual activity that does not inspire the unity of the church is empty, delusive, and vague. It couldn't have been piloted by the Lord of the Church, Jesus Christ! There are many things that leaders of denominations and their lieutenants do that seemingly 'tear' the Body of Christ apart.

These men and women encourage, wittingly or unwittingly, animosity, divisiveness, segregation, and all kinds of vices you can think of. When true revival comes, this shall no longer be so. These unguided fellows will become irrelevant and outdated. The church shall effectively occupy her place in the scheme of things in the nations. The church belonging to Christ is the only body so authorized by God to execute deliverance upon men who are under the tyranny and fiery harassment of the Prince of this world.

How shall the church be able to earnest her God-given potential, except Christ is the only message to the dying world? Christ is the Baptizer and Harvester. It is in preaching His Person that revival erupts! I see many preachers preaching all kinds of messages, some even preach themselves and naively think that that can amount to anything. Look at John the Baptist's confession about Jesus:

> *"I baptize you with water to show that you have repented, but the one who will come after me will baptize you with the Holy Spirit and fire. He is much greater than I am; and I am not good enough even to carry his sandals. He has his winnowing shovel with him to thresh out all the grain. He will gather his wheat into his barn, but he will burn the chaff in a fire that never goes out."* **Matt. 3:11-12** - GNB

Fire is the transmitter of every true revival. You cannot experience lasting revival when fire is absent. Things remain dead and status quo until fire comes into the picture. Thank God for a John the Baptist who knows that whatever he was doing, as important and acceptable by men as it may look, must be submerged by the one and only Baptizer of fire, Jesus Christ. John knows he has limitations to how well he can help men; he deferred to Christ. Can we have men and women who will publicly acknowledge their weaknesses and inadequacy so that the Man of Calvary may step in with His fire?

One of the reasons why revival is scarce today is because of the species of men and women on our pulpits. They have and are still obscuring the Baptizer by unadvisedly turning the focus lens on themselves. Many revivals have come and gone because the men of God became too popular than the owner of the 'move'. They took the glory belonging to Christ and cornered the 'spoils' of revival to make monuments for themselves. The move of God in any generation becomes scuttled when the men around it have become so eager to gather the gains for themselves rather than see to it that it becomes a wildfire.

Once the Baptizer is no longer in charge, men only gather ashes and unfortunately, no matter the amount of ashes packed, it cannot produce fire. It is only good to be discarded. Each minister or gospel worker must know that it is *"...not by might nor by power, but by My Spirit, says the Lord of hosts."* Zech. 4:6

Men who travailed and prevailed with God in their generation knew this truth considerably. This truth kept them moving on in the move of God. These were used and were never staled or discarded by God. I hope that as you are reading this book, it becomes very clear to you that without God you can do absolutely nothing!

No one can bring revival to men until he or she has come in contact with fire from the presence of the Lord and has been thoroughly purged. It is at the instance of fire that the inner condition of a man is revealed and healed. God knows that until you have come under His fire, you are unfit to bear fire among men. Isaiah was a very fierce preacher of righteousness until the Lord revealed to him his own inner life so that he could seek God's help. It was when he was exposed to fire that he knew he was doomed without God's help.

When God confronts you with the issues of your life, it is not to condemn but that you might see your helplessness and as a result, seek God's help earnestly. The challenge for many is this lack of personal self-examination and evaluation. If there is anything the devil likes to do all the time, it is blindfolding men from seeing issues correctly. I tell you the truth, because it is easy to go into error, hence the need to regularly check your standing with God (2 Cor. 13:5). Now, until a man regularly examines himself, it becomes difficult to repent properly before the Lord. Of course, there is a difference between being remorseful and true repentance.

One is said to be remorseful when he or she feels disappointed with himself or for particular wrongdoing or for failing others. Whereas, repentance is a godly sorrow borne out of the conviction that one has wronged God or has fallen below divine expectations. Meaningful repentance that is fruit-yielding is when you have taken full responsibility for your wrongdoings and thereby seek God's forgiveness and help.

This genuine repentance was missing in Eli seeing his untoward attitude toward the misbehaviors of his two sons – Hophni and Phinehas. They were flagrantly contemptuous against the holy things of God. Hophni and Phinehas were *children of Balial*; they were thoroughly sacrilegious. Could you think of anything evil they did not do as they conducted their priestly duties? Eli's sin was his refusal to be stern with them despite all the warnings from God to him; he was nonchalant. Eli and his two children died the same day just as the Lord had said beforehand.

Are you also being warned by God my brother? What has been your attitude to the correction of God over your life? Have you simply moved on or grown so cold toward God as though He had become too repetitive? It is not wise for you to continue to patch things up and continue in hypocrisy when in reality you need revival. Don't allow arrogance to deny you the help heaven would have graciously released unto you if you cry out in repentance. Check what the word of God says:

> *"My son, do not despise or shrink from the chastening of the Lord [His correction by punishment or by subjection to suffering or trial]; neither be weary of or impatient about or loathe or abhor His reproof, for whom the Lord loves He corrects, even as a father corrects the son in whom he delights."* **Prov. 3:11-12** - AMP

It is not negotiable, God's servant must be weaned and separated from every form of filthiness so that he can be exclusively God's. When revival comes, it purges and purifies. All the impurities are removed in the instance of fire. As you are being exposed to punishment or training under God, it is like being put under fire! It is never pleasant on the flesh at any time, yet it is what builds godly character. I do not see how anyone can truly become a child of God without being subjected to thorough discipline under God.

> *"If you aren't disciplined like the other children, you aren't part of the family."* Heb. 12:8 - GNB

Discipline must precede ministry. It shouldn't be the other way around. Many ministers think that what gives credence to ministry is spiritual gifts. We now have a species of preachers who are morally bankrupt yet can demonstrate 'power' gifts. This is not correct. Character (godly) is what builds ministry and not gifts. The biblical pattern of ministry that will know starts first in the place of character formation before graduating into the manifestation of power.

Look at Samson who never paid attention to his consecration. Character formation was omitted in his life, so it didn't take long before his 'fire' was put out by the enemy. Man of God, why are you so much in a hurry to go and start something when the issue of your discipline has not been sorted out with God? If you hope to last in ministry, your confidence should not merely be anchored on spiritual gifts and eloquence but more importantly on whether you have been formed.

God does not commission a man who lacks the kind of fire that is contracted in the place of formation. Some people carry 'strange fire' around; only God knows where they get it from! It is not everyone who is seemingly 'blowing hot' that is carrying holy fire; beware! Any fire that does not draw men to repentance is but a strange fire.

A man becomes an instrument God can use to ignite a fire in the life of others when he has become 'fire-full'. It takes a revived life to revive another. There won't be energy to do the work of God acceptably and effortlessly until you have experienced a genuine revival within.

> *"And he stretched himself out on the child three times, and cried out to the Lord and said, "O Lord my God, I pray, let this child's soul come back to him." Then the Lord heard the voice of Elijah; and the soul of the child came back to him, and he revived."* **1 Kings 17:21-22**

The boy in the above story was completely dead. Life has been snuffed out of him. It was such a hopeless situation! And you can imagine the agony in the heart of his widowed mother. It was awful enough that she was a widow and more devastating was to lose her only child. What can she possibly do with a dead child? Her was needing urgent divine intervention.

Thank God for Elijah who carried such an intense "fire" in his life that a lifeless boy could be resuscitated. This man of God saved the day because he possesses fire! We need fire to savage the rottenness that has come upon us in our day. Dearth and deadness cannot operate where a man who carries fire is on duty. Elijah saved the woman and her son from dying for lack of food caused by famine in the land. May you become the answer to the cry of your generation in Jesus' name.

Revival is bringing back to life what was dead. It is the reawakening of the soul. But it does not come when it has not been earnestly sought after in the place of prayer. God is the one who can make it happen by His Spirit. It is neither an event nor a program that can be organized for optics. The purpose of every genuine revival is to bring men to seek God and become intimate with Him through the transformation of their hearts. A man becomes useful and useable in facilitating revival in others when he has been purged and carrying the fire from God's presence. No divine commissioning until all the filths are gone leaving only godly character needed for life and ministry. Until Isaiah arrived at this point, God did not commission him even though he had been in ministry.

You need revival urgently when you are no longer pricked at the instance of sin, you need a revival when you are no longer zealous for good works, and you need revival when you are lukewarm in the place of prayer. What is the condition of your life? Speak to the Lord about it now!

CHAPTER
3

# Followership: God's Method for Divine Incubation

*"And as He walked by the Sea of Galilee, He saw Simon and Andrew his brother casting a net into the sea; for they were fishermen. They immediately left their nets and followed Him. When He had gone a little farther from there, He saw James the son of Zebedee, and John his brother, who also were in the boat mending their nets. And immediately He called them, and they left their father Zebedee in the boat with the hired servants, and went after Him."*
**Mk. 1:16-20**

*"And Jesus, walking by the Sea of Galilee, saw two brothers, Simon called Peter, and Andrew his brother, casting a net into the sea; for they were fishermen. Then He said to them, "Follow Me, and I will make you fishers of men." They immediately left their nets and followed Him. Going on from there, He saw two other brothers,*

> *James the son of Zebedee, and John his brother, in the boat with Zebedee their father, mending their nets. He called them, and immediately they left the boat and their father, and followed Him."*
> **Matt. 4:18-22**

When you look at this story closely in the two renditions, there was a man called Zebedee, he was the father of Simon Peter and Andrew. He had trained both of them in the business of fishing and he also had servants. They were on their fishing business as usual until Jesus came along and called the two sons to follow Him to make them "fishers of men". The Bible said they left what they were doing and followed Him immediately.

I imagine the queries that could be running through their father's mind, "How could you carry my two sons in one day: First, I don't know you and secondly, I don't know where you are taking them." But his children followed without questioning from that day onward. Now, the matter for me is what He told them – "*follow Me, and I will make you...*"

## Intentional Followership through Discipleship

> *"And seeing the multitudes, He went up on a*

> *mountain, and when He was seated His disciples came to Him. Then He opened His mouth and taught them, saying:"* Matt. 5:1-2

The scenario in the above Scripture might look ordinary but I don't want you to handle it as such. Multitudes followed Jesus everywhere just as His chosen disciples also did. The Lord does not discriminate against anyone so far there is the willingness to come to Him. Jesus needed to teach despite the thronging crowd and so climbed the mountain. It looked to me that the Lord gave everybody an equal opportunity to come to Him as He climbed the mountain, but surprisingly only His disciples climbed to meet Him when He was seated.

I noted that Jesus didn't call His disciples to come up; they did on their own volition. It appears the Master was testing the selection He had made, by not inviting them officially to climb along with Him. They knew they were to follow Him everywhere He went regardless of the terrain. Their class for that day was a very tedious one; that teaching was so elaborate and deeply concentrated that it took about three chapters in the book of Matthew. It was intended to expose them to the kingdom lifestyle.

The Lord was and still is not biased; if the multitudes had left the valley for the mountain, they also would have had that first-hand experience as did the disciples. Many so-called Christians today are permanent valley dwellers and are reluctant to climb since it involves going the extra mile or making sacrifices. How can someone ever think he can follow Jesus without inconveniences? Human beings are naturally inclined to comforts and that explains why they stayed back in the valley.

Correct following would normally involve climbing onto the mount. If you must turn out well in His hands, you must be willing to go all the way as He leads. The Lord does not leave any stone unturned for His disciples to turn out well; He does not compromise His dealings with them at all because He truly desires their triumph. It is on the mountain that intense concentration of thoughts, prayers, and instructions take place. Serious spiritual impartation does not take place in the valley because it is mostly populated by those who are undecided. What usually keeps men in the valley is the desire for personal ease and self-indulgence.

Yes, God will come to the valley mainly to recruit followers but He does not make or commission them there. Every following should cascade into a discipleship relationship with the Master. Even though God is Omnipresent, He dwells in the secret place and not in the public domain. This by implication meant that those who will be made by Him must be ready to be with Him even if it involves being in obscurity.

> *"And he ordained twelve, that they should be with him, and that he might send them forth to preach."* Mk 3:14

When Jesus ordained the twelve to be with (follow) Him, it is that by so doing, He can make them into what they have been destined to be in life – "Fishers of Men". God won't make a man by pursuing him around; He sits on him unobstructed. Look at a mother hen for example: she does not lay her eggs in the open where every passer-by would have access to it. The process of her mating might be public but the laying and incubation are usually behind the scene.

The mother hen looks for a spot where she would not be disturbed by any external interference and then lays her eggs. For the first few days or weeks, she might be going in and out for food but as the days draw closer to hatching, she stays put. She will not mind starving herself so that she can give maximum concentration ensuring the eggs turn out well. This is referred to as the incubation process!

The incubation period is a very critical moment that should not be tinted with insouciance. It is between life and death! Do you know one or two of the eggs can roll out misguidedly beneath the mother hen or be touched by a human hand? Once this happens, such an egg or eggs become useless; they cannot be consumed as table eggs or become chicks by any means. When broken, it is repugnant and capable of contaminating the air. No matter how hasty the mother hen wants to be, the period of incubation can never be shortened otherwise she comes out emptyhanded.

In the same manner, there is a divine incubation. Jesus incubated on all His disciples and you can attest to what happened to them all except the one that rolled out. It is in following Jesus that you have the opportunity to be divinely incubated. The followership that I am talking about has no resemblance with the kind of movement we see all around today all in the pretext of following Jesus. That was the kind of followership Judas Iscariot engaged and it never profited him. We shall take time to look at the practical ways of following Jesus not too long from here.

## "...And I will Make You"

> *"Then He said to them, "Follow Me, and I will make you fishers of men."*
> *They immediately left their nets and followed Him."* **Matt. 4:19-20**

There are several instances in the Bible where God had promised to make a man, and every time He vocalizes that intention, He doesn't get overcome by that willingness and then forgets to put forward the terms and conditions. God is never frivolous at doing anything at all. There is no hide-and-seek with God; He makes the terms and conditions very conspicuous so that it does not appear as though you have been cheated or tricked into doing something you are averse to or unprepared for.

No man in himself is sufficient to take on divine tasks; he must need to be transformed first. It is upon this truth that submitting to God for making becomes very exigent. Although men in their nature for one reason or another do not like to wait or willingly submit to the formation process; they are usually very hasty. God is never in a hurry to send anybody out to represent Him until He is assured that a transformation has occurred in that life. One of the virtues to be learned is patience.

The tendency to misrepresent God is a sure possibility when you have avoided or evaded the requisite making. There is a divine making that must take place in your life and the Lord is asking if you are willing and prepared to go through that heat. Many have gone out to do God's work when in an actual sense have not gone through the incubation and the hatchery processes. That's why we see all kinds of things everywhere all in the name of ministry today.

The disciples were exposed to several issues and these became the basis and platform for their learning and making. Some lessons, they learnt in a hard way and others easy but quite instructive. Thank God they followed on and that's why they were able to learn. It is as you learn that you can become; nobody becomes anything tangible if he has not been so taught and learned. Though learning can be very rigorous, there is no substitute for it. Again, who you learn from is very critical and determines what becomes of your life. Jesus categorically said that:

> *"A pupil is not superior to his teacher, but everyone [when he is] completely trained (readjusted, restored, set to rights, and perfected) will be like his teacher."*
> **Lk 6:40** - AMP

It is as God deals with you through different experiences in your discipleship relationship with Him that you are made. Many believers erroneously think becoming a "mighty" vessel in the hand of God is exacted by a mere ritual Bible reading; embarking on a long fast or until the hand of one 'anointed' man of God is laid on them. Others suggest that what makes one fit for ministry is the certificate obtained from a seminary or a theological school. Now, I am not condemning any of these, but the truth is that no man can be made just by observing any of these! No one is made by God through Spiritless routines.

God is the one who designs and determines the curriculum of each disciple's training leading unto making. His dealings are peculiar and unique to each individual and so a correct disciple would not need to compare Christ's dealings with him with another disciple's. You will discover that even though Jesus had many disciples that followed Him everywhere, He had unlimited space in His heart to relate with them individually (see Peter in *Jn. 21:15-25* and Thomas in *Jn. 20:19-20, 24-29*). Jesus' dealing with one did not short-change or rob the other. That's the graciousness of my Master; He is inexhaustible and available to all!

But then the Master does not force Himself over anyone; He won't barge in on you to assume your "teacher" or "maker" when you have not voluntarily conceded the authority to so do to Him. When Jesus called the disciples to Himself, they also had the right to delay or outrightly turn down the invite. I thank God that "they immediately left their nets and followed Him." They left what had occupied them for years and was going to make them nonentities as far as God's purpose for their lives was concerned. They abandoned the net of limitation and mediocrity for the surpassing worth of divine making.

What is that net that has kept you disobedient and unyielding to the hand that desires to make you? That net could be your age-long methodology of doing ministry, it could be that relationship that is leading you to nowhere, or it could be a particular mindset that is not Christlike. For another, it could be a habit; temper, or besetting sin. Yes, that net may even look harmless, appear legitimate, or still, "resourceful" in your evaluation; if only you can see that it is just a broken cistern that can never hold water. I wish you heed His voice as He calls you to come aside and be made into something supreme.

The making of a man by God does not take place overnight; it does not happen spontaneously as most men would wish. God does not do "touch and go" to suggest that a precious article can be made in just one contact. Something that is meant to be durable requires maximum contact otherwise it becomes inferior and disposable. God is not in a hurry just to produce anything. He waited patiently for forty (40) years to get Moses "send-able". Are you feeling that you must jump out now to do something for God? Can I ask you to wait for divine launching instead of going around introducing yourself to men?

Divine launching takes place when the period of divine incubation has been completed and hatching has taken place. It is during your making that God will pour Himself into your life through numerous instructions that will eventually become lively in you. You will notice that some of the instructions Jesus gave the disciples were given while they traveled alongside the Master; some were given amidst the crowd and others privately. They were exposed to all kinds of terrains: mild, moderate, and extreme. It was intentional so *"that the man of God may be complete, thoroughly equipped for every good work."* 2 Tim. 3:17

## The Church's Role in the Making of Men

The church ought to, by God's design, facilitate the making of men through discipleship. But it yet appears as if today's church is not strong enough to produce genuine disciples out of men at her disposal. She seems to be dabbling into many things outside her primary calling. Deplorably, no matter how seemingly nice and plausible those things are, they remain mere distractions and can only lead nowhere.

Look at all kinds of "jokes" happening in the church of Jesus in our own time! The church now has the similitude of a *bazaar* where all kinds of wares are exhibited for buying and selling. One thing is sure: The Lord is set to depose all the "moneychangers" and "miscreants" that are obscuring His purpose in the hearts of men through their evil deeds even if it is called ministry.

We must understand that the church is both the bride and exclusive property of the Lord Jesus Christ. No man, dead or living is qualified to own or appropriate her for personal prominence. It's a dangerous ambition and destructive enough for anyone to pursue. God is still very protective over His church. Those who have dealt treacherously with her didn't find it pleasant. At a time, these men and women seem to be everywhere but have now been forcefully shut down. God is the sole Owner and to Him alone, the virtue and glory of the church belong.

The church is meant to conceive, birth, and nurture lives till the Person of Christ is known and formed in them through genuine biblical discipleship. Men cannot be made to fit for eternal purpose outside an informed church. What do I mean by an informed church? It is a church that knows and understands the essence of her existence as so intended by God. Jesus was speaking and describing what an informed church is as recorded in the book of Matthew:

> *"Simon Peter answered and said, "You are the Christ, the Son of the living God." Jesus answered and said to him, "Blessed are you, Simon Bar-Jonah, for flesh and blood has not revealed this to you, but My Father who is in heaven. And I also say to you that you are Peter, and on this rock I will build My church, and the gates of Hades shall not prevail against it. And I will give you the keys of the kingdom of heaven, and whatever you bind on earth will be bound in heaven, and whatever you loose on earth will be loosed in heaven."*
> **Matt. 16:16-19** - NKJV

> *"Simon Peter spoke up and said, "You are the Anointed One, the Son of the living God!" Jesus replied, "You are favored and privileged Simeon, son of Jonah! For you didn't discover this on your own, but my Father in heaven has supernaturally*

> *revealed it to you. I give you the name Peter, a stone. And this truth of who I am will be the bedrock foundation on which I will build my church—my legislative assembly, and the power of death will not be able to overpower it! I will give you the keys of heaven's kingdom realm to forbid on earth that which is forbidden in heaven, and to release on earth that which is released in heaven."* **Matt. 16:16-19** - TPT

It is in the above Scriptural passage the word "church" was mentioned for the very first time in the Bible and it came directly from the mouth of the Lord Jesus Himself. When the Lord was talking about the church, He was not in any way conceptualizing an inanimate or physically built temple, sanctuary, or a place of worship for that matter; He meant human lives. The church is a community of believers, who have made Him clearly their Lord and as expected have cut every tie with sin, self, and the world system with all its allurements.

The modern-day church is stuffed with different kinds of people who lack the rudiments of the Christian faith. It is very worrisome that men and women grow in ranks but not life; very religious but not led or controlled by the Holy Spirit. Undoubtedly, the church that Christ is coming back for must be *spotless* and without *wrinkles* otherwise, she stands the risk of being rejected. There are a few other issues we still need to quickly pick from the scripture reference whilst still looking at what an informed church should be.

Again, an informed church is one that seeks above anything else the knowledge of Christ. She prides herself in the revelations of the Son of God that come to her ceaselessly. That's when she is truly a Bride so adorned with glory, grace, and light. What makes her desirable and bear rule in the nations is not earthly fabricated but heavenly. Her power and significance on the earth is her uncompromising union with her Bridegroom. And that's what the devil had always targeted; to pull her away from the One that makes her beautiful and powerful.

Second, the desirable church is by nature harmless as a dove yet militant in her living. Though gentle, she is perceived as radical because of the undying affection she has for her Bridegroom – Jesus. All the arsenals in heaven are at her disposal if her one and only pursuit is to see her Lord known and enthroned in the hearts of men on planet Earth. We have too many merrymaking and fun-seeking churches in our day that are either ignorant or just averse to true spiritual knowledge.

Sadly, the kingdom of darkness is having it cool; never roughened or threatened since the present-day church is so overtaken by a mere show of exaggerated and ostentatious lifestyle.

Are you seeing the way our children are exiting the church as though they are looking for something else that the church couldn't give them? They are now being hired by the world system not only to oppose but to also ridicule the sacred faith handed over to us by our founding fathers. All these are effects of the backslidden church of our day. Many are confused because there seem to be no clear-cut instructions as to what Christianity is and why the church is in the first place. They perceive the church as a waste of time or a common monastic lifestyle.

As long as we continue to parade an uninformed church, it will be practically impossible to subdue the whole earth for Jesus; the darkness that has engulfed the earth cannot be overturned by this mere show and empty faith profession that is void of Christ-like light. Instead of bringing savor to men, it will only plunge them further into distasteful living. The church won't be spared from being trampled upon by men and women she missed the opportunity to affect. Hear what Jesus says:

> *"You are like salt for the whole human race. But if salt loses its saltiness, there is no way to make it salty again. It has become worthless, so it is thrown out and people trample on it."*
> ***Matt. 5:13** - GNT*

Until the church has taken her rightful place, she cannot conceive talk less of delivering men for God's eternal purpose in this generation or any other. A lot lies with the Church; a generation is deemed fortunate or otherwise depending on the state of the church in that dispensation. The early church produced several lives that stood out in their generation. Men like Stephen, Barnabas, Timothy, Aquila, Priscilla, and a host of others were fruits of the devoted church.

> *"So the word of God spread. The number of disciples in Jerusalem increased rapidly, and a large number of priests became obedient to the faith."* **Acts 6:7** - NIV

The early church experienced the power of God because of her utter devotion to the doctrine of Christ. True growth, both numerical and spiritual, only emanates from the ministry of the undiluted word of God. Church growth that is not occasioned by the truth of God's word is but a fluke and lacking substance. Anything else you use to gather a crowd other than the word of God will soon finish and the people will "scatter" from you. It is the doctrine of Christ that possesses the power to keep men on the journey to eternity.

I see how some so-called men of God are now employing all kinds of gimmicks including threats, empty assurance of miracles, brainwashing, hypnotization, and feeding programs, to say the least just to pin men down for themselves. This is wickedness and I am wondering where they have learnt it from. Jesus never used anything else apart from the word of life to hook men for

God. He didn't approach or seek any man for Himself or His ministry other than for God.

> *"Do you not believe that I am in the Father, and that the Father is in Me? What I am telling you I do not say on My own authority and of My own accord; but the Father Who lives continually in Me does the (His) works (His own miracles, deeds of power)."* John 14:10 - AMP

This is the secret of an enduring ministry that can produce the species of men God is looking for to permeate the whole earth. We should have known by now that any departure from this Christ's pattern will only produce unstable men whose frame and living are not wholly controlled by the Holy Spirit.

## Stages of Making in Discipleship

Let me reiterate here again that men are truly made only through the instrumentality of discipleship. It is practically impossible for someone to become a fine and choice vessel for God without having gone through this process. Give me any man or woman throughout the Bible who became notable, useable, and durable for God and I will show you such one was a disciple indeed. You may not find it anywhere in the Old Testament where the word

"Discipleship" was used but the principles were copiously practiced.

Abraham, Moses, Elisha, and Ruth to say the least all fulfilled the conditions of discipleship. Look at the conditions so explicitly stated:

> *"Then Jesus said to His disciples, "If anyone desires to come after Me, let him deny himself, and take up his cross, and follow Me."*
> **Matt. 16:24**
>
> *"Then Jesus said to His disciples, If anyone desires to be My disciple, let him deny himself [disregard, lose sight of, and forget himself and his own interests] and take up his cross and follow Me [cleave steadfastly to Me, conform wholly to My example in living and, if need be, in dying, also]."* **Matt. 16:24** - AMP

Ruth as an example in the Old Testament submitted to God in discipleship under her mother-in-law, Naomi. Her marriage to one of the sons of Naomi came to an abrupt end when the young man died. This unpleasant event gave her sufficient reasons to go back to her former gods and people (Moab). She is now free and young enough to pursue something else just like anyone in her situation would. But Ruth would not do that; she forfeited her right to go back by choosing Jesus and cleaving to her mother-in-law.

> *"But Ruth said: "Entreat me not to leave you, or to turn back from following after you; For wherever you go, I will go; And wherever you lodge, I will lodge; Your people shall be my people, And your God, my God. Where you die, I will die, and there will I be buried. The Lord do so to me, and more also, If anything but death parts you and me."* Ruth 1:16-17

Don't be tempted to think there are no attractions in Moab to go back to, otherwise Orpah would not have kissed Naomi goodbye. Despite the attractions and 'prospects' in Moab, she chose to suffer with Christ rather than enjoy the pleasures of sin there. Looking at the statement of the Lord Jesus in *Matt. 16:24*, one would see that Ruth met the conditions of discipleship. She disregarded, forfeited, and jeopardized her interests and benefits in other to follow God under the hand of Naomi. Death was not a big issue for her at all; she took up her cross when she let go of her ambition to follow God. This is common to all those who walked with God in discipleship.

Discipleship is a means by which a believer can be made to fulfill eternal purpose. Jesus said *"...follow Me, and I will make you..."* (Matt. 4:19). That ship that conveys men from the natural realm unto spirituality is discipleship. The Captain of this ship is the Lord Jesus Himself.

> *"Then he told them what they could expect for themselves: "Anyone who intends to come with me has to let me lead. You're not in the driver's seat—I am."* **Lk 9:23** - MSG

The blunder I see many believers commit today is the desire to lead while the Lord standby to take their orders. It is common to profess the lordship of the Lord Jesus over their life but far from it in reality. This is a lack of discipleship! Had they been raised in discipleship this kind of demeanor would have been very strange amongst those called by the name of the Lord.

Let it be abundantly clear that discipleship is voluntary; God has not and will never coerce or cajole anyone into it. All the men who followed Jesus were never pressured or threatened to do so. The same still applies today and perhaps may be the reason why many hesitate to submit their necks to the yoke of discipleship.

Discipleship is a period of incubation, wounding, and forming. The daily death that every child of God must experience is only possible whilst following Jesus in discipleship. I do not see how any man can follow Jesus meaningfully without bearing the cross that crucified Him. It is when we appropriate His crucifixion that we can truly experience victory over all that made men stumble.
It is good to desire preaching of the gospel, but you cannot preach the Lord effectively when the daily crucifixion has not become your personal experience. It is the crucified that can preach and

serve the crucified Lord. The pathway to this daily crucifixion is DISCIPLESHIP.

## Learning Christ From Other Disciples

One of the reasons why Jesus came into the world in human flesh and lived among men is that the Person of God may be made known to them. Aside from God's Act, a very critical thing to learn about God is His Way. He would all men know His way. How is it possible for anyone to know God when he has not been directly taught? How can a man live acceptably before God when he has not seen anyone lead that life before him? Getting to know God is never a mysterious thing as some mischievous fellow would make it seem; the order is to desire it and then be taught.

A disciple is and remains a learner throughout his lifetime. What and from whom does he take his lessons for in living? Yea, from Christ – the Author and Finisher of the precious Christian faith (Heb.12:2). Christ is both the Subject and Teacher at the same time. All that a disciple needs to learn and know about life and ministry, are all packaged in Jesus. The disciple is never disadvantaged, not even once for choosing to learn from Christ.

Many believers think they would become inferior, obsolete, or even push-aside compared to their counterparts in the world should they completely defer to Jesus for their daily living. This is a great error to think Jesus is only relevant within the four walls of church buildings. Whereas all the men who affected their generation secularly or otherwise were able to do so because they carried the Spirit of Christ wherever they operated. The government of their days came on their knees as well as the hostile generation in their time.

God lived among men through Jesus to reveal what an approved life looks like. Without the help of God directly inputted into a man, he cannot live to please God no matter how he tries. That help personified is JESUS. It was His death and resurrection that brought the *New Creation Life* into being. It is this kind of life that can become like Jesus and also mirror Him. This life is the one that brings fragrance to God's nostrils. Howbeit God wants it spread everywhere instead of the unprofitable human life!

Of a truth, this new life from Christ may have been born in a believer but has not become experiential yet in his daily walk. It is as he is being trained by another *older brother* in whose life Christ is conspicuously living and reigning that he is taught and assisted. The experience of young believers today is punctuated with more failures than successes in walking the new way. This is so because he seems to be lonely and deserted; no one is holding his hands! Everybody seems to be busy with other more 'pressing' kingdom matters than travailing upon babes until Christ is formed in them. Laboring upon men can be very toilsome and that explains why only a few people are fully engaged in it!

This 'touch and go' ministry that is prevalent in our days cannot produce the kind of men God is looking for. Those who will perpetuate the move of God at this end time would be those who someone has labored on deliberately and concertedly. We must as a matter of urgency and with alacrity begin to raise men whose passion and enthusiasm to learn Jesus is second to none. This of course can't be done outside discipleship. But then only those who are themselves learning Christ can be resourceful to others.

> *"He said to them, Therefore every teacher and interpreter of the Sacred Writings who has been instructed about and trained for the kingdom of heaven and has become a disciple is like a householder who brings forth out of his storehouse treasure that is new and [treasure that is] old [the fresh as well as the familiar]."* Matt. 13:52

The solution to the harassment and disgraceful things happening all around us lies in the learning of Jesus. Misbehavior is what we have indirectly bargained for when the Man of Calvary is not the Teacher or the Subject taught. When one gives his or her life to Christ, truly he becomes a new creature in Christ Jesus according to the Scriptures. But it doesn't just stop there; the new life that has begun has the need to be nurtured and brought up by being exposed to the Person of Christ otherwise it is exterminated leaving behind a form. The devil is never happy that a new life has been born to the family of God, hence with great indignation seeks its ruin and termination.

## Practical Ways of Learning Christ From Other Disciples

Life begets life. Right from the beginning God commanded all creatures to produce after their kind. This command, as it applies to material things, so does it apply to the Spirit; *"...and that which is born of the Spirit is spirit."* Jn. 3:6.

Without a doubt, imparting another life spiritually entails maximum contact. Nothing of the Spirit is bequeathed casually to another life; it is by deliberate and concerted labor. Both teacher and pupil must be ready and willing to be sacrificial. No matter the availability of the discipler, until a disciple is willing and open to learning, nothing much is achieved in their discipleship relationship together.

Discipleship must be life-on-life training aimed at learning Christ. It starts by observing other human lives in discipleship. The apostles learned Christ by being at His disposal all the time; they were with Him twenty-four hours a day and seven days a week observing and learning Him. It is as they follow and observe Him that His life is being transferred to them.

On every platform of human interactions, discipleship is found practicable. Whereas other religions follow a particular routine and ambient but not so with Christianity which is discipleship-based. Every moment of functional discipleship is orchestrated from heaven. There is no mistake or coincidence; everything is so planned to follow a curriculum designed by the Master Himself as long as the disciple is ready and yielding.

Many times, a disciple may think he is just relating with his discipler and forgetting to note that behind that human hand, is the Lord's. A disciple needs to watch it lest he is hampered in his walk with God because of his lack of understanding. Christianity that is not drawn from following (discipleship) after Jesus' pattern of living is but a mere religion. Discipleship that does not see Jesus every day cannot be assessed as one.

As a discipler, there is nothing wrong with your disciples living with you so that the life of Christ can be seen as touchable and livable through your life. Discipleship is not only in teaching; it also entails others seeing and doing. How beautiful as an artisan that those apprentices under you have become disciples who are learning Christ apart the vocation either at home or in the workshop. So, the environment you live and work becomes your natural habitat for your discipleship. It is more real to learn Christ in natural environments where there is neither pretense nor acting.

Discipleship in its naturalness does not give room for dualities, where, present in one man are different characters and personalities. It is dubious when an individual, regardless of where he is, has an unstable life. He may be a saint in the church but a sinner elsewhere. Such a person is never a disciple of Christ.

When discipleship has succeeded in a life, there shall be an undeniable character formation. Something deep has happened both inside and outside that cannot be mistaken! What strange kind of Christianity that is everywhere now and spreading like wildfire; it tones down on godly character as evidence of salvation! How can somebody be a Christian yet clothed with sin and self?

As the apprentice relates with his master either at home or in the workshop, he can assess first-hand, the livability of the life of Christ in the master and then the possibility of contracting that same life. He can draw instructions for his life either positively or negatively.

## Physical Birth

Discipleship involves physical contact and interactions. Everyone who has been physically born has what it takes to disciple or be discipled. The learning process is possible because one is physically born. We cannot be talking about a process where there is no basis. Physical birth is very crucial in proceeding to discipleship. One needs to be born first and thank God you have been born.

The story of the young man in the Bible came to heart - Mephibosheth. He was born into the royal family of Saul as an able-bodied but became lame because he was not properly handled. None is created to be useless but for the ineptitude of those who handled them. Even if a man is destined to be a king, it will be so if such life is handled by correct 'midwives.'

For the fact that you have been physically born and not a stillbirth, the truth is that you have the potential to become a disciple in the hand of Christ. Jesus Christ had a physical form and was taught both physical and menial things by His parents as He grew. He grew just like any child would. He didn't live as a spirit, but as a man and among men. So, the physical birth of a man is very crucial to becoming a disciple of the Lord.

Discipleship is not limited to learning and growing in spiritual things but in physical things also. Our parents as designed by God are to disciple us in physical things such as home training. They are your initial handlers in discipleship. They can also be called midwives unto discipleship. So, when parents are not available for the children in physical discipleship, something will be wrong definitely. That's why you see several children today who lack basic social decorum and moral standards because their parents omitted the training.

The parents have the responsibility of guiding the children to correct living such as how to dress well, basic table manners, personal hygiene, etc. These are the initial training process in discipleship at home. Once a man has experienced physical birth, he can become a correct disciple under the hand of the Master.

## Spiritual Birth

You may have experienced the first (physical) birth, without a spiritual birth you can never become a disciple of Christ. In *John 3:3*, the Lord confronted Nicodemus with the issue of spiritual birth. Permit me to call him Bishop Nicodemus; he had a staggering profile. He was a leader, a giver, he was so versatile in the Law of Moses, he was a nice man and a very serious-minded Pharisee. All of these qualities were not sufficient for Jesus to be quiet about the need for spiritual birth. The Lord simply told him; "You must be born-again." Bishop Nicodemus was shocked because Jesus knew His deficiency. He asked several questions that looked childish for a man of his religious attainment.

Nothing of the Spirit takes place in the natural man. He may have sincerely tried; it's just that he has no capacity for such. Except the old gives way, the new cannot spring forth. The natural life has to be evacuated to make space for the new life. It is this new creation life that can be discipled and become like Jesus. Let me liken the process of evacuating the old life to the quarry site experience. If you have been to the quarry site, you will allude it's not a quiet place.

As there are all kinds of machines at the quarry, so also are different sizes and shades of stones there. Those machines are used to crush stones into desired shapes or sizes. It is a noisy place because a whole lot of crushing, cracking, and breaking takes place there. If the stones can be used in their rough form, who will bother taking them to the quarry? Stones are naturally not malleable, except compelled by a superior force. It remains shapeless until there is a chiseling. This process of cutting does not happen without quaking which will generate noises. If you ask those stones, they would have preferred to be left in their former state!

That is what God does to every man who desires a walk with Him in discipleship. He will subject you first to the quarry site experience which is to cut off the naturalness in one's life. The wisdom of God is that every noise and breaking should have taken place at the quarry site so He does not expect any breaking that will constitute noise in His temple. Look at the wisdom of God in 1 Kgs. 6:1-7, *verse 7* in particular:

> *"And the temple, when it was being built, was built with stone finished at the quarry so that no hammer or chisel or any iron tool was heard in the temple while it was being built."* 1 Kgs 6:7

The life that is heading unto perfection in Christ Jesus must have been to the quarry site where his human nature is expected to have been crushed having collided with the cross otherwise it becomes almost impossible to bear the nature of Christ. There are all kinds of noise in the sanctuary of God today because one way or the other, men evaded or escaped the quarry site experience. How do you explain one church taking another to court and then the unrighteous will judge 'helping' them to settle their differences employing the empty wisdom of the world? It's the lack of quarry site experience that is responsible for this abysmal.

There are two managers: I call the first one, the *quarry manager* and the other, the *temple manager.* The temple manager for example requests three 3 by 2 stones to the quarry manager to fill a space in the temple. By implication, the quarry manager will do a lot of chiseling, breaking, and crushing to meet that specification. You know stones are not all the same sizes, some are shapeless and thereby need to be chiseled to meet the requisition.

If there is no quarry experience, there can't be a temple experience. As the quarry manager begins to work to get *3 by 2 stones*, there will be cracking and crying. No matter how disturbing the noise is, the quarry manager does not stop. As the stones are crying, the manager seems to say "No quarry experience, no temple experience." In divine incubation, I see a lot of crying underneath. You might be bleeding under a human discipler, he will say sorry and continue to cut, chisel, and hammer until Christ is formed in that disciple.

A discipler may act as a quarry manager depending on what God is doing par time in the life of the disciple; the temptation is to think that the discipler is being wicked – No don't think like that, it is to bring out Christ within your frame! Of course, discipleship is not to recruit people to do domestic chores for the discipler even though it is not wrong that disciples help the discipler out with that once in a while, but they must see you do it first, it is part of learning Christ. Discipleship must never be seen as slavery but as an avenue to learn Christ's life.

Every discipler has the responsibility of being an audio-visual aid to everyone around him and in particular those God has put under him for learning. Love and compassion must readily be demonstrated in your life. When your wife is complaining that you don't love her, she is simply asking you to show the love of Christ that you profess.

Don't shut her down by looking for a way to get back at her by withdrawing privileges from her. How have you resembled Christ by this your action? Even as a wife, why should you demand for something in return before fulfilling your conjugal responsibility towards your husband? But that's what prostitutes do and you are not one. We have not so learned from Christ!

Will you allow God's hand to mold you? Stop running and dodging His hand from forming you. If you desire God's help for your life, you must yoke yourself with the Master in discipleship. There is a need for you to turn your life to a human discipler if you hope to go far in the purpose of God for your life. I have a discipler also whom I am learning Christ and also reporting my growth to. I have been disciplined once or twice by him and I am grateful to the Lord for such privilege.

So many people have passed under our hands, some learned Christ very well and others ran away. It is not strange they left; men ran away even from the Lord. Jesus was never embarrassed because they made that; He even permitted the twelve in case they would also like to go away. Discipleship, even though it is voluntary, is the ship that will take you to God's presence when you close your eyes in death. God is not a tyrant; He leaves you to make your choice.

It is always good, my brother, to have somebody that you have submitted to in discipleship; an elder who can call you by your name without adding a title or any of such not to disrespect you though; one who can pull your ear and you won't feel embarrassed or diminished. Many are lone rangers today, they have nobody they report to, who can call them to order, what a pity! When you are a lone ranger, you can do anything even when those things are not correct because nobody to correct you.

All the eyesores that are being perpetuated in our midst today are a result of a lack of biblical discipleship. Many of our leaders are already lords and they 'know it all'. They report to nobody; they are under the scrutiny of no one. Whatever they say stays and nobody must check even when it is unfounded scripturally. Those following are unrelentingly gullible while others are as stubborn as a mule.

If only you will allow God to form your life in discipleship through another life. Will you prayerfully allow God to point a human life to you that you can submit to simply to learn Jesus and you will thank God for it? I have enjoyed and still do because God placed me under a man whom I am learning Christ from.

By the grace of God, I also have disciples everywhere that God has graciously released to us to labor over until Christ is formed in them. One of our sisters who submitted herself to discipleship under God's leading was told to move from Lagos to Maiduguri in Bornu State.

She obeyed and relocated even when she knew no one there. This sister was single at the time she relocated. To cut a long story short, that single obedience to God that discipleship brought to her was what brought her where she is today. She got married to a man who loved the Lord. They have children and are both doing well under God. If she had rejected to be discipled, only God knows what would have become of her today.

Friends, don't frustrate the hand that wants to form you. Amos 3:3 *"Can two work together, unless they are agreed?"*. You cannot walk with the Master except you have embraced discipleship and the conditions. Though discipleship is learning and walking with Christ, it is yet voluntary all the way. Jesus won't force any man to follow Him.

Discipleship thrives when agreement exists between the Master (Jesus) and the disciple; it is when you have agreed to follow that the journey will be meaningful. In following, there could be rising and falling, but the good thing should be that in the end, you followed through.

CHAPTER
*4*

# The God of Establishment

Let's read from Rom. 8:29-31:

> *"For whom He foreknew, He also predestined to be conformed to the image of His Son, that He might be the firstborn among many brethren. Moreover whom He predestined, these He also called; whom He called, these He also justified; and whom He justified, these He also glorified. What then shall we say to these things? If God is for us, who can be against us?"* **Rom. 8:29-31**

From the scripture above, two words are important for our discussion - "foreknew" and "predestined." "Foreknew" means to have previous knowledge of something or to know an event or happenings beforehand. The word "predestined" is made up of two phrases joined together. "Pre" means before, and "destine" means an end, intention, or ultimate end. "Foreknew" and "predestined" can be used interchangeably. In the context of the scripture above, we can safely say that "predestined" means what is in the heart of God before one's birth or before anyone ever knew you.

Remember what God told Jeremiah in *Jer. 1:5*, that before Jeremiah was formed, God knew him; God has a purpose for him, and there is an agenda in the mind of God concerning him even when he had never existed. So, you see God affirming His knowledge of Jeremiah even before he was born at all. God knows you, don't go about as if He does not know you. Even the things you don't know about yourself yet, only Him knows. He knows every man and woman no matter where they are. It is foolish for any man to think he can hide from the Lord; even if you are inside a hole, He can see you very clearly.

I visited Canada many years ago. My older sister is married to a Canadian, and they were celebrating their 30th wedding anniversary. We all went out for dinner with their daughters. When it came time to order wine, my sister chose one for me. I made sure to read the label to confirm it was non-alcoholic. While I was doing that, one of the daughters asked her father if I was a saint because, for her, consuming a small amount of alcohol was not a big deal.

Now, it's much easier for me to have a sip of that wine and freshen my mouth, especially when I am far from home as if my consecration is only necessary where I can easily be recognized. Do you know, when it's time for my niece to get married, she insisted that I officiate their wedding in holy matrimony because she saw a light life in me. Without the help of the Lord, the temptation to misbehave when you are in an unfamiliar place is very strong; something whispers to you, 'Let go now, you are far away after all.'

## God's Great Plan for You

Every man who is currently on planet Earth or just arriving has all that he needs in life set aside by God before he or she was ever born. God has also allotted time to every man or woman; none of us has the luxury of eternity on this side. So, you must be quick with the program of God for your life. Don't waste your time, eternity on the other side is knocking. It will be totally unfortunate to enter into eternity with a sense of guilt and nonachievement of the purpose of God for your life!

According to Rom. 9:11-16, ever before the two boys were born, God had already ordained how their lives shall be. What God ordained for a man; he does not need to struggle with it. God is absolute and can never be faulted in His counsel and purpose. Whatever God has ordained or purposed for a man can only manifest if such a man cooperates and has faith in God that whatever He has purposed is the best for him; it is at that point he progresses and enjoys God's dealings onto actualization of God's purpose.

Many are struggling in life today because of the blatant ignorance or unyielding attitude they exhibit towards God. Rejecting or limiting the involvement of God in your life allows the devil's devastating blows to land on you. Look at all the mess men had to go through for being double-minded. Some are so harassed in their sleep that they have no other choice than to stay awake by attending compulsory church vigils just to escape another assault from the enemy. Human nature, being what it is, prefers making sacrifices to simple obedience and these sacrifices don't come cheap.

> *"Samuel said, "Which does the Lord prefer: obedience or offerings and sacrifices? It is better to obey him than to sacrifice the best sheep to him."* 1 Sam. 15:22

Unfortunately having to go through the extreme rigors of making sacrifices does not spare or pardon any disobedience against God. Some suppose that subjecting their bodies to certain stringent routines will bring in the much-desired peace of mind; they are wrong. You can be sure that the devil is never playing around. He is a serious business-minded individual whose eyes won't be distracted from the target — to *steal*, *kill*, and *destroy*. The most sensible thing to do as a mortal man is to throw your life trustingly at God Who has a track record of not failing; not even once! You must trust God totally for liberation.

When you are not walking in the path of righteousness, the manifestation of God's purpose in your life will be slowed down and delayed because only *"...the people who know their God shall be strong, and carry out great exploits."* (Dan. 11:32). There are many things that God has predestined for you; to be established in them requires you walk in God's counsel. Can you check if you are still in the center of God's will for your life?

As a child of God, your establishment should be all-encompassing. It is not good that you are established in one area and not in the others. Such a sign of spiritual imbalance makes you an easy target for the enemy. The wicked one will not be able to do anything about your life if Christ is well seated in your heart.

Some time ago, in the middle of the night, I heard this terrifying noise that was not ordinary; it was a combination of several animal cries and that of a newborn baby. That incident should have aroused needless and fearful prayers, but as far as the *One who keeps Israel never sleeps or slumbers*, I had nothing to worry about; I just went back to sleep. There is an inner life that is not troubled in times of trouble; this kind of life is firmly connected to heaven round-the-clock. So, I say to you with authority that no harm can come near you if you are well-rooted in Christ.

When God has established a man, he flees from every appearance of sin. Such a man has zero tolerance for sin and any form of unrighteousness, no matter how insignificant or imperceptible the act may appear according to human standards. Many of our brethren struggle with sin and self because they have not seen or understood the Person of God. God cannot tolerate sin, no matter how little you may consider it. It was for sin that He turned His eyes away from His beloved Son, who knew no sin but drank the cup into which our sin was poured. It was Christ's painful death on the cross that brought about our sure victory over sin thereafter.

Until you have seen the powerful transaction that took place at the cross and has personalized the gains it brought to humanity, living a victorious life over and above self and sin remains far-fetched. The greatest setback that man has ever known is the self-life. He is simply ignorant that he can never be established by himself. The more he tries to advance, the more he is deepened in confusion and satanic bondage. Hell is always empowered and ahead of every effort conducted by human energy in whatever endeavor. The enemy has great fear of the cross because he is aware that it is the instrument by which his puppet (sinful human life) is terminated.

Living a crucified life can be done absolutely by faith through the power of the Holy Spirit. The strategy of the devil is to veil the hearts of believers from seeing and trusting in the work done at the cross. It is his highest delight to see Christians erroneously wanting to walk with God outside the Holy Spirit-revealed cross through faith. However, no one can please God without faith in the finished work at Calvary. It is faith from the standpoint of the cross that makes one unshakeable and undefeatable by the world system.

> *"For every child of God defeats this evil world by trusting Christ to give the victory."* 1 Jn 5:4 - NLT

Regardless of how fierce the battle against the righteous may seem, victory is certain if their connection to Christ is firm and pure. Many believers do not know that binding the devil is not the first thing to do when facing difficult times, but to check if their spirit is healthy and securely connected to that of the Lord. There is no need for all those long 'prayers' and empty tongues or all these overzealous church activities when you have yielded your ground to the enemy. You've to retrace your steps back to the cross!

The wife of a certain so-called man of God traveled, leaving him and the children at home. During her absence, the man brought his girlfriend into the house. Despite this, he continued his usual practice of praying with the children in the morning and evening. Unable to tolerate this hypocrisy, the woman sought out the church where he worships, questioning the audacity of the man to continue to preach and act as if he were upright. Have you seen the wickedness that is ongoing in our churches today? Now, wouldn't it be better for him to expose himself to God before he is exposed to the whole world, with the accompanying shame and disappointment?

The Bible instructs believers to see themselves as dead to sin following the death and resurrection of the Lord Jesus. Until the revelation of what transpired at the cross vividly plays in their hearts, they have yet to experience victory over sin and self-life. It is only when this has happened that they are truly able to be of God. When one sees oneself as dead, sin no longer has power over them, as *"For he who has died is freed from sin."* (Romans 6:7). Just like when you slap a dead man, no matter how many times, he does not retaliate because he is dead.

When you carry Christ within you, you will be firmly established in all aspects of your life. God will not allow you to go through needless embarrassment. Remember the incident when Jesus was seized and asked to pay taxes? He instructed Peter to go to the river and catch the first fish he found, and inside it, there was enough money to cover both their taxes. By walking in righteousness with God, you will never find yourself stranded in life.

You may not possess great wealth, but what is needed to sustain you will always be provided. True prosperity is not about material possessions but having unrestricted access to God's presence. If you have God within you, even those who possess worldly riches will bow before your God. Ahab being the king couldn't pin down

Elijah, the man of God. Elijah sealed the heavens for three and half years and there was no rain until he said otherwise. We need men of God like Elijah today, who will not tolerate unrighteousness for anything in the world; not those that have corrupted themselves with the king's portions. These so-called men of God have become tainted and lost the grace to speak out against evil. People may still respect them, but do they truly have a place with God?

Except God has established you in contentment, you will eat all kinds of things, including poison. Many people are struggling with their lives because of what they ate, all in the name of serving on the "altar". A well-instructed believer should know that he is called to a life of sobriety; not for pleasure or ease is he living for. He is alive not to pursue personal agendas, no matter how plausible, but as a vessel through whom Christ may be made manifest. It is an aberration that the one who has been redeemed would glory in any other thing apart from the cross. Look at the confession of our brother Paul:

> *"But it's unthinkable that I could ever brag about anything except the cross of our Lord Jesus Christ. By his cross my relationship to the world and its relationship to me have been crucified."*
> ***Gal. 6:14*** *- God's Word*

Is it not disturbing to see a child of God having the same drive to own possessions as the men of the world would? Did the Lord not show to His disciples what their attitude should be towards the goods of this world? Many presume Jesus came, died, and resurrected to empower their lustful appetite for a 'good life' in this world. This is not so. That some so-called men of God are sponsoring covetousness in the hearts of their followers does not change God's verdict about the world and how a believer should approach it!

> *"Do not love the world or the things in the world. If anyone loves the world, the love of the Father is not in him."* 1 Jn. 2:15

Jesus came to give us eternal life — the God kind of life. A life so distinct from the impoverished and possessive human life we inherited from Adam. God is so eager to see this New Creation Life permeated in every man. Its perpetuity has nothing to do with how many material things it possesses. Its nourishment and satisfaction transcend the earthly goods. It is a life that owns nothing yet lacks nothing! (2Cor. 6:10). The Lord talks about Himself being the true Bread of Life that comes from heaven. Anyone who is a new creation desires Jesus' flesh more and more; they derive great satisfaction from consuming it.

How do you know a worldly believer? He desires more worldly goods than he would the Bread of Life. He desires more money in his pocket than more of Jesus in his heart. This kind of Christian places earthly gains far above spiritual gains and honestly the more physical gains the less spiritual he becomes.

> *"The ground covered with thistles represents a man who hears the message, but the cares of this life and his longing for money choke out God's Word, and he does less and less for God."*
> **Matt. 13:22** - *LB*

The truth is that there would always be contention between God and mammon. People crave more money because it is believed that it turns desires into reality; it affords more goods in the world. Where God is truly held as the Lord, mammon is considered insignificant, and vice versa. Anywhere money becomes a major consideration in doing the work of God, you can be sure God is not glorified! He will distance Himself from such work.

Do you see the kind of recognition that is rendered to mammon in our time? As mammon is reinforcing its lordship in the world, it is also negotiating its enthronement in the church. Consider the messages delivered from our pulpits regularly; they imply that the main benefit of serving God is financial gain.

One day, a woman approached me after a service, asking for prayers so that those who owed her money would repay her; it seemed she was a business owner. I prayed as she requested. The following Sunday, she returned with a bag, intending to give it to me. When I inquired about its contents, she excitedly exclaimed, "Pastor, your prayer worked! All the people who owed me have been paying back one by one, so I have come to appreciate you." I declined the money, instructing her to use it to pay her tithe and invest in her business instead.

Over the years, I have learned not to hastily accept things from those whom God had not started eating from; those I have not labored on and whose growth is now apparent; and those who are not yet disciples. You know as I rejected the money brought by the woman, something said to me “Remember there is no soup in the house, be wise” Thank God I didn't obey that strange voice. Many of us have not done well in this regard; we are too eager to collect goods from men that we are not sure of their salvation and relationship with God. You will pretentiously 'bless' a sinner and release him to continue in his wickedness.

The Lord is not interested in what a natural man can give but in the redemption of his soul. How many so-called men of God have squandered the souls of men who should have become a gain to the kingdom of God just because of their belly problems? God is displeased!

Years ago, a woman donated a car to a church without consulting her husband. When he returned from his journey, he was informed that the car had been given to the church. To everyone's surprise, the man asked for the car to be returned. As a result, the church had to give back the car, now in a better state. This awkward situation could have been prevented with more careful consideration when accepting gifts.

## Bliss in your Matrimony

> *"In the same way you wives must submit yourselves to your husbands, so that if any of them do not believe God's word, your conduct will win them over to believe. It will not be necessary for you to say a word, because they will see how pure and reverent your conduct is. You should not use outward aids to make yourselves beautiful, such as the way you fix your hair, or the jewelry you put on, or the dresses you wear. Instead, your beauty should consist of your true inner self, the ageless beauty of a gentle and quiet spirit, which is of the greatest value in God's sight. For the devout women of the past who placed their hope in God used to make themselves beautiful by submitting themselves to their husbands. Sarah was like that; she obeyed Abraham and called him her master. You are now her daughters if you do good and are not afraid of anything. In the same way you*

*husbands must live with your wives with the proper understanding that they are more delicate than you. Treat them with respect, because they also will receive, together with you, God's gift of life. Do this so that nothing will interfere with your prayers."* **1Pet. 3:1-7** - GNT

God being the One who institutionalized marriage created it for the total enjoyment of the man and his wife. Many are married today and are oblivious of what their marriage is meant to achieve. Some consider it a necessary evil while others find it fashionable. Yet none knows how to marry and stay so except he/she has been taught by God. A blissful marriage is not automatic; certain lessons and know-how had to be learned from the Manufacturer Himself otherwise the effect would be colossal. God must be given a free hand to establish your marriage on His sure and ageless counsel.

The relationship of a couple (a man and a woman) cannot be conducted on the altar of ignorance; they must both seek with all seriousness to know the purpose of God for their union. It is utter confusion when you seek to engage and enjoy a gift while snubbing the Giver. Marriage is a gift to man and remains the sole idea of the Almighty. I see many people wanting to apply carnal methods to what is spiritual; they fail to understand that marriage is spiritual and can only be approached with spirituality.

# Pay Attention to that Foundation...

God of establishment will not preserve anything He did not lay the foundation. Whatever is borne out of the natural will never be owned or claimed by the Spirit. There are too many things that people parade and nurse hoping that such things will receive God's blessing when in fact He did not *know* their come-about. Like Abraham, they like to *force* God's hand to bless Ishmael He didn't conceive or initiate. But you can be sure that He can never be coerced or coned to validate what is not divine.

You must mind the foundation of your marriage. Sister, why will you compromise and start a relationship that God never sanctioned with that man? Are you seeking to secure a marriage at the expense of open heaven over your life seeing the way you are going about it? You need to think twice! Everything may seem alright now, but that's how it normally looks until you get into the middle of the ocean and then discover you are stuck.

Brother, will you take the counsel of God to go and *sleep* until God says to you *"It is not good that the man should be alone"*? I see how you go around sisters in the fellowship causing confusion with your empty "vision". You can't have a good marriage foundation like that. If you think you will catch a wife like that, no you will only catch trouble!

Every foundation that is hurriedly laid is a disaster in waiting. Do you see how rapidly marriages are collapsing these days? The reason is not farfetched — wrongly laid foundation. When the foundation is faulty, what can anybody do other than to go through the pain of going back to it to make every necessary correction? Though the process of digging around it is not usually palatable, it is not negotiable. God is never a careless builder or one who is hasty to do something. Whatever He does is definitely to last forever. Let us confirm what the word of God says:

> *"I know that everything God does will last forever. You can't add anything to it or take anything away from it. And one thing God does is to make us stand in awe of him."* **Eccl 3:14** - GNT

It is most unreasonable for anyone to expect that a thing whose foundation is not built by God should last even when it looks promising. The efforts that have been put into such a venture won't count if God's involvement is missing. Though that thing may look dazzling and captivating, it's going to end up in the dungeon eventually.

Have you discovered a fault or compromise in the foundation of your marriage? The way to go about it is not to patch it with all kinds of visages, it is to come out and be helped by God. Instead of pretending as though all is well, why don't you cooperate with God to visit that foundation and make it right?

It is when He has established your marriage that the two of you can even agree and walk together in all things. How many husbands ride their wives like slaves and then the wives come up with all kinds of things in self-defense? Some husbands are unusually caring to their wives when they are looking for sex and terrible when they are to give money for the house upkeep. This is not godly.

Your wife is not a slave or 'help-mate' but a 'help-meet' for you. One of the help any man can receive from God is his wife. When as a husband, you recognize the role of your wife in your life, you will do well in life and ministry. God has packaged your wife to suit your peculiarity.

When a man fails to appreciate the fact that it is favor that brought a wife to him, he misbehaves and treats her anyhow. Now, this is a foundational issue! If such a man has been walking with God, how would he not recognize that his wife is an integral part of his life?

I recall a time when my wife traveled abroad for two months, and I had to cook by myself. The kitchen I had been using regularly suddenly became too big and unfamiliar to me. I found myself calling her frequently to ask where she had placed things in the kitchen. I was amazed that even from afar in the UK, she could still remember all the *little* details of where she kept what in the kitchen. We should be grateful to God for our wives!

When the husband is sick, the wife is sick; when her man is troubled, she is troubled alongside. Some men do not care what happens to their wives; sometimes she is not feeling well but her husband can still sleep and snore, may the Lord have mercy. God is the witness to all the mistreatments against her. Many husbands are struggling today because God is the one resisting them simply because of the way they have dealt with the wives of their youth. Prayers remained unanswered; offerings are a waste when God is unhappy with him for dealing coldly with his wife.

> *"And this you do with double guilt; you cover the altar of the Lord with tears [shed by your unoffending wives, divorced by you that you might take heathen wives], and with [your own] weeping and crying out because the Lord does not regard your offering any more or accept it with favor at your hand. Yet you ask, Why does He reject it? Because the Lord was witness [to the covenant made at your marriage] between you and the wife of your youth, against whom you have dealt treacherously and to whom you were faithless. Yet she is your companion and the wife of your covenant [made by your marriage vows]."*
> **Mal. 3:13-14** - AMP

Has the Lord found you guilty in the way you conduct your matrimony? When you are *found wanting* in the balances as God weighs you, who can plead for you than to make the necessary correction? Instead of your long prayers and unending fast, would you be humble enough to give your wife her rightful place in your life? God desires to establish your home as a specimen for others to emulate and follow. There is no reason for any marriage if the purpose of God for it is lost.

As a husband, it is your God-given responsibility to make room for the spiritual growth of your wife. Don't stiffen the environment that should have enhanced her blossoming. A correct leader does not rival with his subordinates but rather goes ahead giving direction for them to follow. Christ being the ideal husband pursued the growth of the bride (the church) deliberately until her glory burst forth. With patience and longsuffering, He labored for her purity and maturity. The virtues that sprouted were not achieved overnight; they testify to the consistent sacrifices of the Lord. This love displayed by Christ was what brought the church to the place of prime and glory.

Christ laid down His life for the church and by that has given us an example of what it means to be a husband. Being a husband is a great thing and comes with serious responsibilities; it is a trust given to you by the Lord and to Whom you shall give account of your stewardship. The Lord Jesus in Matt. 19:3-11 brought great clarity to the misconception the Pharisees had about marriage. They came intending to trap Him, as usual, to see what answer He would give to their question about the issue of divorce. It was as

Jesus was answering their premeditated question that we got to know that marriage is not just a mere thing; only those it has been given to by God can accept it (vs *11*). No man should go near it if he is not ready to be accountable to God. Marriage hinged on law, human traditions, and even societal norms and beliefs can never stand except the one based on God's counsel.

The wife is not to be relegated to the background though she is expected to *submit to her own husband* according to Eph. 5:22. Undoubtedly, it is in her submission to her husband she sees and receives blessings. Who her husband is wouldn't be a precondition for her submission. Though she is married to a drunkard, her submission to him must be unwavering. As she humbles herself beneath her husband's authority, such a gesture is unto the Lord primarily.

> *"In the same way you wives must submit yourselves to your husbands, so that if any of them do not believe God's word, your conduct will win them over to believe. It will not be necessary for you to say a word, because they will see how pure and reverent your conduct is. You should not use outward aids to make yourselves beautiful, such as the way you fix your hair, or the jewelry you put on, or the dresses you wear. Instead, your beauty should consist of your true inner self, the ageless beauty of a gentle and quiet spirit, which*

> *is of the greatest value in God's sight. For the devout women of the past who placed their hope in God used to make themselves beautiful by submitting themselves to their husbands."*
> **1Pet 3:1-5**

Do you see why Christian marriage is completely different from that of the world and why it is not meant for all and sundry? Marriage is far beyond human intelligence; in fact, engaging natural sense only gets it weakened. How can one explain that the beauty of a wife is in her submission to her husband? That is the wisdom of God and it is superior to that of humans. A true wife is known by her total submission to her husband as unto God.

Not cosmetic or superficial wives would God use to push His kingdom agenda amongst men. When a wife is too artificial and has her eyes on the desire to look beautiful at all costs, she would by all means lack the requisite space in her inner man to handle spiritual things. She does not yet understand that what makes a woman beautiful is not the labor on the outward but on the inside. It is a fact that a cosmetic wife has her heart too narrow to conceive talk less birthing the deep things of God. Such a wife will not be able to contribute substantially eternal values to her husband.

The worth of a spiritual woman is beyond measure. May the Lord bring forth wives are spiritual in our homes in Jesus' name. The impact she carries is profound. She has transcended the immature and worldly ways that characterize other women. Only a spiritual woman can genuinely submit to her husband because her submission is rooted in her relationship with God.

A truly spiritual person is never arrogant as it is not a characteristic of the fruit of the Spirit. When a wife is genuinely spiritual, she never struggles to submit to her husband, which can be quite glorious. Every righteous and knowledgeable husband, working in harmony with God, actively seeks the spiritual development of his wife until it becomes evident in her character.

Husbands, don't leave your wife behind while you are running to grow your roots downward; ensure she pursues her personal spiritual growth too so that she does not become a needless burden to you. As much as God looks for the oneness of your spirits, He earnestly desires much more that each should find his or her depth in Christ Jesus. Each should support the growth of the other, but one cannot grow for two; the need for a personal walk with God is very critical.

The value of a wife transcends cooking, sex, and childbearing; she is made for more and indeed a great asset in the hands of a correct husband. Unfortunately, not many husbands know how to tap into the inherent resourcefulness of their wives. She can be likened to gold that is covered up in mud; casual, careless, hasty, and unskillful hands can't discover talk less to bring it to a refined state. A lot of work goes into that. If you like to see your wife break forth, you have got to labor on her concertedly and deliberately. I see several men struggling with their wives today and will even blame her for their supposed 'ill luck'. They are in error! Instead of threatening your wife go and learn how to become a real husband from the Lord.

The value of a wife transcends cooking, sex, and childbearing; she is made for more and indeed a great asset in the hands of a correct husband. Unfortunately, not many husbands know how to tap into the inherent resourcefulness of their wives. She can be likened to gold that is covered up in mud; casual, careless, hasty, and unskillful hands can't discover, let alone bring it to a refined state. A lot of work goes into that. If you would like to see your wife break forth, you have got to labor on her concertedly and deliberately. I see several men struggling with their wives today and will even blame her for their supposed 'ill luck'. They are in error! Instead of threatening your wife, go and learn how to become a real husband from the Lord.

Every husband desires his wife should not disprove him but has he honestly earned that? Have you proven yourself to be followable over time? Have you treated her as a very important integral part of you? Have you honored and respected her both in secret or public? Now these are the few things amongst many others that compel her to follow you and at the same time give the necessary environment for her breaking forth. In addition, they engender growth, progress, and togetherness under God.

To see a man and his wife hold their hands while walking together openly for true affection in this part of the world is very rare. This is chiefly so because many couples are not so cordial and our culture considers such scenes as either being unserious or unnecessary. I once witnessed a heartwarming scene in Atlanta where an elderly couple showed affection towards each other. Despite their age, they remained deeply connected. To maintain a strong relationship, certain intentional actions are necessary to keep you united.

A Christian home is the one patterned after Christ's relationship with His church. You are not doing well if your home is not mirroring Christ yet. Our marriages are meant to perpetuate the move of God on the earth. The enemy of righteousness that plunder the first marriage must not repeat his victory in your home. God's wishes for you as a family are good; He likes to see you move together in unity and oneness. It is of no benefit for God to see His children scattered and shattered. He likes to see you established.

When the relationship between a man and his wife is cordial under God, it means they have been established. Does that mean they don't disagree? No, they may disagree many times but because they both cherish God's fellowship and friendship, they settled. How many homes are in disarray because they have not been established in God?

# Obedience: Key to Your Establishment

God of establishment loves those who will walk with Him in obedience all the way. Obedience means to be completely yielded to God; it is letting Him have total control over the whole of you. It involves laying down your all on the altar of sacrifice. It takes a humble heart to obey God. The company of those who are obedient to God is a treasure to Him. The test of our love for God is in our obedience to His word. He would not accept delayed obedience from anyone; incomplete obedience does not establish anybody; it is the same as outright disobedience. Every genuine prosperity streams from prompt obedience to the Lord.

No man can truly be established when he is full of himself. You couldn't be an established man when your life is not correct. God does not establish a wrong life. Several lives are in serious desire that God may establish them but for what? When God established a life, it is because that life is useful for divine purpose and program. God considers it no need to bless a man whose planning and pursuit are awkward and averse to kingdom agenda. Brother, what do you want to do with your arrogant heart? How far can you go with your proud way of life? Can you humble your heart before the Lord and cry to Him to perform a surgical work upon your heart such that your establishment can begin?

A man is truly prepared for establishment at the instance of the truth and not psychology. It is God's word that conveys and implants the truth in a man's heart. May we earnestly pray that men will have an encounter with God's word because until then the power to be established is absent. We have seen in our day men who come with motivational and psychological talks thinking that's what men need.

Transformation, which is a necessity, yet lingers if we miss God's word in its purest form. Many things are being said on our pulpits today that resemble God's word but regrettably are not. And so, they cannot establish anyone in the way of the Lord. If you are going to be sincere and truthful with me what has anybody become through that? Our God is not a psychologist!

God does not use His word carelessly as some people suppose. Unlike men, He is neither a liar nor a soothsayer (Num. 23:19). God has no reason to sweet-talk anyone to score cheap popularity or acceptability. He is God; He won't need the validation of anyone regardless of their prominence or worth amongst men. When God says "Beloved", it means to be very loved. The love of God is not temporary; He normally loves to the end. You become the beloved of the Lord when you have conducted yourself strictly in His love. Your lifestyle henceforth is utterly demonstrated as reciprocating God's love. Many profess their love for God but their manner of living says otherwise. How is your lifestyle? Is it well or not?

This love continues to overwhelm a man when he reciprocates God's love with obedience. You never can know the power and the depth of God's love until you yield your life to God completely. A man can shower his love upon his wife just by mere words but lack action. Demonstration of love entails actual action. So, when God calls a man beloved, He means it. God's love for His children is unwavering. He does not love merely by word of mouth. *"...I wish above all things."* (3 John 2). God seeks those whom He will lavishly bring into His ineffable love.

Except the matter of sin in a man's life has been permanently dealt with, he cannot be truly established. Even when a man has been established by God before, he must not now become relaxed around sin; otherwise, he will be uprooted so easily. Sin has audacity and will cripple its victim at any time. When sin is given space, it does not matter where or who you are; it seeks to gain mastery and constantly make demands over your life. You can be in the church and at the same time sin demands that you sneak into a dangerous pornographic website. Sin has neither restraint nor mercy for its victims.

Sin has enough power to disgrace a man. Have you ever wondered why your sinful habits are not letting you go even when it is very obvious that you are harming yourself? It is the tenacity of sin. Those who smoke, for example, are so caught up in it that they don't realize when they have finished a whole packet, even though they started with the intention of just having one stick.

Sin makes no apologies to its victims; it is very audacious! The devil does not stop at just enough when it comes to promoting sin. You can cry and bleed, but your tears do not move him; they instead excite him. If there is anything as sharp as a razor that can cut a man into pieces, it is sin! Being a three-letter word should not make you underestimate its effects because it can be very devastating.

Are you a masturbator? Have you tried to stop, but the more you try on your own, the stronger the urge to masturbate becomes? Do you often find yourself undressing women in your mind and imagining things when you see them?

Are you now twenty-five years old and still unable to break free from this sinful habit? When will you rest and give up this sinful lifestyle? Though you cry day and night to be established, I hear God asking you, "Why and how; have you not read that I cannot behold iniquity"? Don't even try to bribe with empty religious activities; you cannot deceive God. Many are involved in various activities, thinking they can manipulate God to do their bidding, but they are deceiving themselves. Having one foot in God and the other in sin cannot work at all.

It does not matter who is assuring you, saying 'It does not matter; God is not that difficult.' If only you could take godly counsel and move away from such a person. Many people talk about God yet do not know who He is. The Bible tells us,

> *'What shall we say then? Shall we continue in sin that grace may abound? Certainly not! How shall we who died to sin live any longer in it?'*
> **Rom. 6:1-2**

When you sin, you have 'tied' God's hands together and certainly hindered Him from reaching out to you. Do you desire an unobstructed answer to your prayers? Then you must jump into the stream of mercy by confessing your sins before the Lord and trust God to live a daily victorious life over sin. Immediately your sins are confessed to the Lord, His hands are untied, and your heavens are opened. You will also soon discover that even the things that you have not prayed about, but God deems it necessary for your life, He will bring them your way because you have become His beloved by obeying and living correctly.

There is a song that we sing in church that we have almost lost the meaning of. This song is scriptural. It says, “Surely goodness and mercy shall follow me all the days of my life.” It is by grace for goodness and mercy to follow you. If you are within the ambiance of obedience and truth, they must follow you. Matthew 6:33 says, *“...seek first the kingdom of God and His righteousness, and all these things shall be added to you.”* That's the order, not the other way around. You cannot ignore divine principles and order and hope to benefit from it. The Scripture must not be violated.

Strive to become beloved by the Lord. This means you will need to watch over your life. Your life and home must be in order. You cannot be a true leader or pastor when your home is in disarray. How can you mistreat your wife and expect to be beloved by the Lord? A man whose home is not in order has no place being on the pulpit; it's complete hypocrisy. Many years ago, I received a distress call from the wife of a pastor well known to me. Upon arriving, I found her on the floor after being beaten by the pastor. This is unacceptable. How can God work through someone like this?

All kinds of frauds seem to be going on in the church today because we have allowed all manner of drama on the pulpit. It looks as though we are gradually losing the spirit of discernment to know and judge every spirit. When there is no discernment, we are turned to the bush by the wiles and schemes of men. The Bible says we should test all spirits. But it will be extremely difficult to test spirits when those who are to so do are not growing in the spirit. To grow in the spirit will mean you are growing your roots in God's word. Allow God's word to become your life; it must be dwelling in you richly. Until this happens, errors will keep increasing in the hearts of men.

CHAPTER
*5*

# Joseph: An example of A Beloved

**Let's see a man amongst many others in the Bible who was a perfect example of the beloved of the Lord.**

> *"Now Jacob dwelt in the land where his father was a stranger, in the land of Canaan. Joseph, being seventeen years old, was feeding the flock with his brothers. And the lad was with the sons of Bilhah and the sons of Zilpah, his father's wives; and Joseph brought a bad report of them to his father. Now Israel loved Joseph more than all his children, because he was the son of his old age. Also he made him a tunic of many colors. But when his brothers saw that their father loved him more than all his brothers, they hated him and could not speak peaceably to him. Now Joseph had a dream, and he told it to his brothers; and they hated him even more. So he said to them, "Please hear this dream which I have dreamed:*

*There we were, binding sheaves in the field. Then behold, my sheaf arose and also stood upright; and indeed your sheaves stood all around and bowed down to my sheaf." And his brothers said to him, "Shall you indeed reign over us? Or shall you indeed have dominion over us?" So they hated him even more for his dreams and for his words. Then he dreamed still another dream and told it to his brothers, and said, "Look, I have dreamed another dream. And this time, the sun, the moon, and the eleven stars bowed down to me." So he told it to his father and his brothers; and his father rebuked him and said to him, "What is this dream that you have dreamed? Shall your mother and I and your brothers indeed come to bow down to the earth before you?"* **Gen. 37:1-10**

Joseph was beloved by his father, Jacob. Joseph found favor with his father right from when he was born. He was the second to the last born of the family. Since when he was young, he had begun to dream about what God wanted to do with him. Let me first submit that not only did he become the beloved of his earthly father, but he also had a fantastic relationship with God. It is only God's beloved that He shows Himself to. God does not show Himself to truants, the sacrilegious, or scorners. Did you note how old Joseph was when he started a relationship with the Lord, he was a teenager. Is it possible to have teens and youths that would have built a relationship with God right from their tender age? Yes, it is. Joseph was an example. Joseph started dreaming in his childhood. Now, maybe because of his immaturity, he told the dreams to his brothers which made them hate him with all passion.

When the father asked him to go and check on how his brothers were faring, that became the opportunity the brothers had been longing for, to get rid of him. They sold him into slavery, and he became a slave to Potiphar. When you are beloved of Christ, the devil will be after your life, but he can only pursue you closer to the fulfillment of your God-given destiny. All those who love God and are His beloved know that nothing happens to them by accident, either pleasant or otherwise (Rom. 8:29). God is always the One, though invisible, yet always at work in their lives, bringing His good purpose to pass.

When Joseph arrived at the house of Mr. Potiphar, the Bible says God was with him. Can you see the life of a beloved of God, even when in a situation that should bring discouragement to his heart, God still stood by him. Joseph was a very handsome young man; a fine man to behold. Potiphar's wife wanted to have a feel of him. Whenever her husband was out, she would softly mention

Joseph's name and call in such a way that it would arouse any young man. Satan is covetous and greedy over every man who is beloved by the Lord. He lusts after such a man for destruction. Joseph was not deceived by all her affections; all the money and promises she offered didn't capture Joseph's heart; Joseph preferred the affection of his Lord. Joseph kept his heart for the Lord.

When the devil wants to capture a man, he tampers with his heart. A man does not just fall into fornication or adultery suddenly; he must have been falling little by little until ultimately crashing into sin. The heart of such a man would have been tampered with several times without any form of restraint. Brother, you need to be careful; why are you being so reckless with your life? When a man cannot control his eyes, he looks at everything that passes by and allows them a place in his heart. Such a man is looking for trouble.

So, after several allurements from Madam Potiphar to seduce Joseph, and none had worked, she decided to seize and force him to lay with her. On this particular day, Potiphar had gone to work; she must have also sent some of the domestic staff on errands and made sure there was calmness and space to do something. With all her detailed evil plot to get Joseph to sleep with her, all was to no avail as she still faced serious resistance from that young man as before.

One would have expected Joseph, like any other random young man, to succumb to his madam's daily pestering. Every time she came, Joseph repeatedly declared he had his affection only for God – *"How then can I do this great wickedness and sin against God?"* (Gen. 39:9). That was what kept coming out from his mouth. He was essentially saying, "How can I risk His love for this thing you are asking me to do?" This kind of bravery is common to all those who have become beloved of the Lord.

Joseph took advantage of grace to say NO to sin. I often wonder what God did to these kinds of men that made them stand for righteousness. In their days, there were no organized seminaries, mission schools, Bible colleges, and the like, yet they followed Christ. They were not timid to declare their love and allegiance to God even in fierce opposition and threats. My friend, what would you do if your female colleague in the office offered herself to you behind closed doors and insisted that you must have carnal knowledge of her? Are you a young girl who has been mishandled by different kinds of men and as such destroying your great destiny?

The way I see young boys and girls rushing for casual sex; what do you want to do with this now? But the grace of God has appeared to all men, teaching us to say No to all ungodliness (Tit. 2:11-12). Grace is flowing from the throne of God, if only you can jump into it, you shall be helped, triumphing over those terrible shackles that have held you bound all this while. God can establish you in grace, you know.

Joseph must have prayed fervently for God to make a way of escape for him. He would rather bombard heaven than consider the option of burying himself in the sand of self-pity and depression like most within his age bracket would resort to. Others may even contemplate suicide. These days, you scarcely see young people who are so given to prayers like Joseph. They hardly seek God's intervention through prayers when in trouble; they rather get crafty, immature, and daydreaming. They pursue empty strategies over prayers; no wonder their frustration is multiplied.

Of a truth, knowledge is on the increase, but the question is to what extent have they been helped? They "know" many things enough to be plunged into bondage and a terrible self-injurious lifestyle. Any knowledge that is not God-centered will only bring untold calamity and anguish to the people. One of the many reasons why several of our young men are abandoning the place of prayer is to satisfy the lusts in their hearts plus this "know it all" attitude. Whereas, only the humble stay and profit in the place of prayers (Lk. 18:1).

Young man, where do you choose to direct your strength? Your actions today will shape your future—will they lead to glory or shame, success or failure, or being a victor or a victim, a champion or vanquished? Many factors sap the energy of today's youth, with social media being a significant one. How can you face the challenges of your time if you neglect the tools that could bolster your position? Practices like a dedicated life of fasting and prayer, regular quiet time, intentional Bible study, and more can strengthen you. Remember, my friend, do not be overly self-assured and neglect seeking grace through prayer. It is through fervent prayer that true victory is achieved.

Joseph's escape from Potiphar's wife was undoubtedly made possible by the Holy Spirit. As he fled, she cried and screamed, pretending to be a victim as if she sought rescue from a rapist. The devil, always the deceiver, tends to protest when God prevails, resorting to undermining righteousness through blackmail. The ministry of the Holy Spirit is essential in the believer's life, primarily to navigate this hostile environment—the world system.

It is impossible, to say the least, for anyone to survive the present and future atrocities typical of this world. Can you see the evidence of Madam Potiphar—the cloth of Joseph in her hand? It was based on this trivial evidence that Joseph was sent to prison without the opportunity to explain what actually happened; and even if he did explain, who would believe a slave boy over Madam's accusation?

The world is full of injustice and utterly cruel in all its dealings. Joseph was immediately thrown into prison without a fair hearing. The rich and those with affluence are far respected and acquitted even when they are guilty; that's the nature of the world. Righteousness is the least of its considerations in judging any matter. That's why it's a dangerous thing to live here without a functional God's presence in your life; it will be a total mess. The world normally "eats up" its inhabitants. No one should travel this way without a guide since it's very easy to fall off.

The road to your establishment most of the time is never smooth; it could be rough and bumpy. The most important thing is that God is the one leading you. God alone has the requisite wisdom to maneuver in difficult times, so please follow. The road could be full of mountains and valleys, but it's never a problem for the Lord.

For Joseph, even though they cast him into prison, they did not know that they had only put him inside a process; the process of establishment. God had already gone ahead of His beloved to give Pharaoh a problematic dream that nobody could interpret, let alone proffer a solution, except Joseph. While he was in prison, they sent the king's security detail to fetch him. The beloved of the Lord may have been dealt with most cruelly, yet it does not affect his worth and relevance. He is fruitful and of great value!

When Joseph got to Pharaoh, he not only interpreted the dream but also gave counsel to the king on what to do to escape the excruciating effects of the famine that was going to hit the entire world.

Though the men of the world have this over-bloated appearance that looks intimidating, they, without any gainsaying, lack substance. The world is overly incapacitated such that it can neither help itself nor any man to be truly fruitful or divinely resourceful. Look at what the Lord Jesus says: *"You are the salt of the earth..."* (Matt 5:13). *"You are the light of the world..."* (Matt. 5:14). The best the world can come up with is rottenness and darkness no matter how it tries. The convulsion looming during Pharaoh's reign could only be salvaged by Joseph, a disciple, a beloved of the Lord. Make no mistake to think Jesus was talking to everyone; It was His disciples, who had earned the mandate of heaven and divinely empowered to rescue the earth He was sensitizing.

The dream Joseph had many years ago was eventually fulfilled, even though it seemed impossible at first. This young man may have been questioning, whether what he saw would ever come true, while also wondering if God had any interest in him. Look at the Bible passage in Psalms 105:17-19:

> *He sent a man before them—Joseph—who was sold as a slave. They hurt his feet with fetters, He was laid in irons. Until the time that his word came to pass, The word of the Lord tested him.*

God's watchful gaze was fixed on Joseph, yet He delayed exalting him until he was purged of personal ambition and the desire for self-glory. Joseph eagerly shared his dreams with his father and brothers—a natural reaction for someone with such grand visions of kingship. Little did Joseph realize that he couldn't fulfill God's plan until he had been refined through trials. These trials were necessary to extinguish his desire to dominate over his siblings. Joseph experienced suffering and humiliation, which ultimately led him to surrender his self-will, self-confidence, self-power, self-wisdom, and self-importance, paving the way for complete dependence on God. Anyone aspiring to serve God effectively must first have lost self to God.

When his brothers, who had betrayed him by selling him into Egypt, eventually came to buy food due to the widespread famine, they bowed before Joseph without recognizing him. Joseph, being the beloved of the Lord, did not harbor grudges or seek revenge; instead, he forgave them, provided for them, and even returned their money. This act of forgiveness was only possible because Joseph had let go of self-preservation and self-love through his trials. Joseph symbolized Christ, reflecting His life in the Old Testament. He told his brothers, "You intended to harm me, but God intended it for good to accomplish what is now being done, the saving of many lives." Look at a believer with a righteous life even in the Old Testament.

Jesus said, *"To him who strikes you on the one cheek, offer the other also..."* (Luke 6:29). Do we still have believers who are carrying the light and life of Christ everywhere today? What do you do when a bus conductor slaps you on a Monday morning? I hope you will respond with the light and life of Christ. When God wants to establish a person, He allows certain things in the form of tests to come your way so that He can have reasons to establish you. However, most of the time, because we are hasty and not learning Christ properly, we react thoughtlessly and negatively, thus missing the opportunity for our growth. This is why many believers sadly remain stagnant in their spiritual journey.

God has the power to establish a man anywhere; He crowned Joseph in a strange land, where he knew nobody. He had no godfather in Egypt, he did not belong to the royal family, yet he became the second-in-command. What He did with Joseph, He can do it again and again, provided He spots that correct heart He is looking for right inside of you. The Lord strongly desires the prosperity and general well-being of His servants.

> *May my friends sing and shout for joy. May they always say, "Praise the greatness of the Lord, who loves to see his servants do well."*
> **Psalms 35:27** - NCV

This fundamental truth should always remain in your heart: God delights in seeing His beloved prosper. Do not let the devil deceive you into thinking that you are not important to God and that you are alone in this world. The crucial question that requires an immediate answer is, "Have you become one of His beloveds?" That's very important! I have personally experienced God's love in my life. He has been with me ever since I embraced this truth; among other things, my health has been excellent. Despite my age, I have never had to be hospitalized or take overnight bed rest there. As He takes me to preach from place to place, He has been the one ensuring my well-being all these years. Praise the Lord; all glory be to Him!

As we read this story, you might be tempted to think it was an easy event, but can I tell you that Joseph did not know what God wanted to do with his life, but he believed God and let Him lead. You don't have the details of your life, only God does so it is wise to throw your life at Him. Joseph went through the pit, prison to palace; he became the second in command after Pharaoh. He became established in God. It does not matter how long it took Joseph to get to the palace, but God's counsel came to pass. Whatever the Lord has said concerning you will be established, if you trust Him in faith because He is faithful that promised.

As we delve into this narrative, one might be inclined to perceive it as a straightforward journey. However, it is worth noting that Joseph was uncertain of God's plans for his life. Despite this uncertainty, he chose to trust in God and allow Him to guide his path. Similarly, we do not possess the intricate details of our own lives; only God holds that knowledge. Therefore, it is prudent to surrender our lives to Him. Joseph's journey took him from the pit to the prison and eventually to the palace, where he rose to become second in command under Pharaoh.

The duration of Joseph's journey to the palace is insignificant compared to the fulfillment of God's purpose. Just as God's word came to fruition in Joseph's life, what the Lord has decreed for you will also come to pass if you place your faith in Him, for He is faithful to His promises. The Lord is presenting before you the opportunity for establishment; don't be like that small child who will choose candies over a diamond. Bow down your heart and pray earnestly for grace for establishment.

Do you have any questions?

Or need any clarifications?

Did you decide while reading this book?

And you need help on what next?

Write, call, or contact:

**OHIOZUA A. ISAAC**

77a, Bola Ahmed Tinubu Road, Iju-Ishaga, Lagos, Nigeria.

08033005279, 07039981844

isaacohi@hotmail.com

isaacohiozua@gmail.com

www.ingramcontent.com/pod-product-compliance
Lightning Source LLC
LaVergne TN
LVHW050559160826
845677LV00011B/2379

*9789787699133*